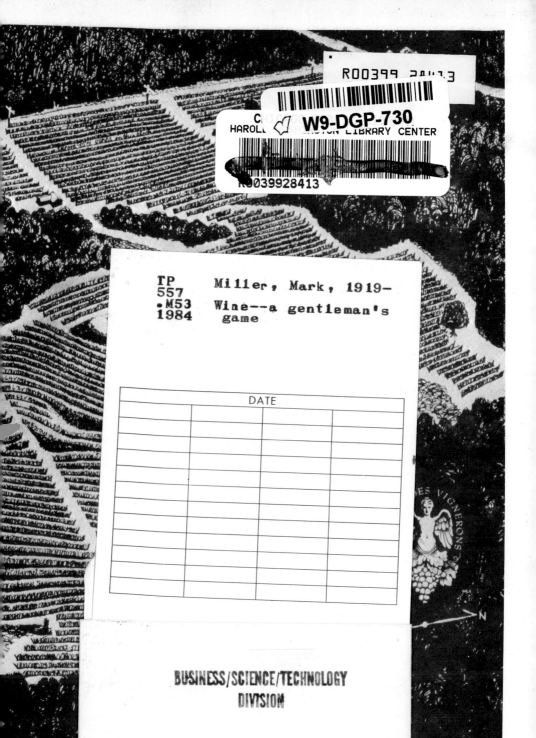

DATE			

Wine - a gentleman's game

1817

**HARPER & ROW,
PUBLISHERS,** New York

Cambridge, Philadelphia
San Francisco, London, Mexico City,
São Paulo, Sydney

Wine - a gentleman's game

The Adventures of
an Amateur Winemaker
Turned Professional
by

Mark Miller

FIRST EDITION

Designed by Ruth Bornschlegel

Library of Congress Cataloging in Publication Data

Miller, Mark, date
    Wine—a gentleman's game.

    1. Benmarl Vineyards. I. Title.
TP557.M53   1983   338.7'6632'0974734   83–47539
ISBN 0–06–015263–X

---

84 85 86 87 88 10 9 8 7 6 5 4 3 2 1

Contents

Introduction

"Le vin, M'sieur Meelair, c'est un . . . violon* . . . un jeu de
. . . comment l'exprimer en anglais . . . Wine ees a genteelman's game."

It was 1963, and Roland Thévenin, a prominent Burgundian winegrower, and I were sitting before the massive
rustic fireplace in the kitchen of his lovely old Château de
Puligny-Montrachet. I had just returned to our rented home
in Burgundy from a trip to Benmarl, my vineyard in America, and had brought back with me a few bottles of an
interesting experimental cuvée of wine grown and bottled
there. I had poured us both a sample and we had been
carefully tasting for a long while. . . . He lifted the glass in

*Violon d'Ingre—hobby.

1

his hand and held it idly against the soft lights of the fire. "Oui, c'est bon . . . excellent . . . mais . . ." The subject was not really just the wines of my little Hudson River vineyard. We had drunk them together many times. "I like eet," he would say, "you could even sell eet en France, but . . ."

What we were actually talking about was economics and the "but" with which he hedged his compliment was meant neither as a criticism of my wine nor a comment on my own middle-class Oklahoma origins. Roland knew that I was growing weary of my constant traveling as an illustrator and that, in spite of what might have seemed an idyllic kind of life, painting glamorous people, working in the most exciting capitals of the world, living in famous vineyard regions in the summer and the Riviera in the winter, I longed to return to Benmarl and devote all of my time to growing and making wine.

He also understood that I made my living from my painting and that when I laid down my brush my income stopped. He was concerned that I perhaps did not understand the financial implications of my yearnings. "Oui, c'est okay comme violon, *but,* mon cher ami, can you afford it?"

The Benmarl Winery sits atop a hill overlooking the Hudson River. From the winery and from our home, which is just across the courtyard, we can look down across some thirty-five acres of terraced vineyards toward the river and beyond to the rolling hills leading to the Berkshire Mountains. In the distance sits a monastery with a red tile roof, reminiscent of those that can be seen in many parts of France or Italy or Spain.

We never tire of this view. The changing light and weather reveal the many moods of the Hudson Valley—still and soft at dawn, gray and brown in winter or cloaked in brilliant snow, vibrant green and blue in summer. At times it is misty, at others obscured by fog or squalls. More often, winter and summer, it is sunny. It is never the same twice.

My most frequent reaction to this landscape is to think

to myself that I must paint the moment, catch the mood on canvas. And then I remember that I am no longer a painter, but now a grape grower and winemaker. Painting, which was once my profession, is now my hobby. My former hobby, wine, is now my profession. At such times, it amuses me to reminisce about how I, along with my wife Dene, born during Prohibition and raised in the cotton and wheat country of Oklahoma, came to live and work on this hilltop.

Every year, thousands of people from all parts of the world come to visit us here at Benmarl, among them the many good friends who have encouraged and supported us through their association with Benmarl's Société des Vignerons. All of them have the same abiding interest in wine. Most of them have traveled through the wine regions of Europe as well as those of California.

Some who come for the first time are seeking help in finding land which they too can turn into vineyards. There have been so many of these, in fact, that at one time we handed out a mimeographed sheet listing the names, addresses, and telephone numbers of local real-estate agents. Some are content to enjoy the life of a *vigneron* vicariously through membership in the Société, and to enhance their own understanding of all wine as the result of their intimate relationship to a working vineyard and winery. Others go on to establish vineyards and wineries, either here as our neighbors or in other parts of the country.

Many people are attracted to us initially, I think, by the romance of the idea of owning a winery and producing one's own wine, and by the thought that perhaps they, too, can have a second career or a change of lifestyle. Making wine is one approach to an alternative lifestyle—one based on independent endeavor in a rural setting.

Today, approximately one-half of the wineries in the United States are organizations which produce less than 100,000 gallons of wine annually. Most of these are family concerns, many of them the effort of a husband and wife. A large percentage of these new ventures have been established within the last ten years. Our story began more than twenty-five years ago.

The estate now called Benmarl has been planted in grapes since well before the middle of the 1800s, making it the oldest continuously operated vineyard in New York, probably in the United States. For the last twenty-five years it has belonged to us—Dene and Mark Miller. We renamed it Benmarl—two Gaelic words which describe the site, "ben" meaning hill, "marl" meaning a slaty soil composition. Its present form is the result of our long love of wine, our personal experiences as *vignerons,* and the wonderful years during which we lived in the heart of the great vineyards of Europe and especially those of Burgundy. The warm people there permitted us to be woven into the fabric of their daily lives, which were totally concerned with the

growing, production, and selling of wine. From these marvelous people, whose station in life ranged from *paysan* to
titled *patron,* we learned to be completely and unself-con-
sciously comfortable with the enormously varied pleasures
which only wine affords.

I think they would be puzzled by Americans' awe of
wine and more so by our willingness to make gurus out of
experts, whom we allow to tell us how and what to drink.
"On n'peut pas demander comment boire. Goûtez! Goûtez,
vous-même, voir si le vin est bon!" they would probably
say.

We set all this down here—the triumphs, the hardships,
the heartaches, the surprises, the romance, and the magic—
with the hope that this little story will help to answer the
questions we are so often asked about how we did it, and
why we did it. We've woven in some practical advice on
what's involved for those who are contemplating a similar
adventure today.

For those among our readers who like to drink wine,
talk about wine, and read about wine, we hope this will
enhance your understanding of a complex subject and
deepen your love of wine.

chapter I

The Road to a Dream

I can't recall exactly how or when my fascination with wine
started, but Dene says that she decided to go out with me
a second time because on our first date I ordered a bottle of
wine with our dinner. She was nineteen and I was twenty-
three, and apparently that bottle of wine created an aura of
glamour that intrigued her. At the time, I was an art student
in Los Angeles. My choice of an art career did not have the
enthusiastic support of my conservative family back in
Oklahoma. From their point of view, it was clearly my duty
as the eldest son to help run the family farms, and they
tolerated my errant pursuit of art only in the certainty that
it would become as clear to me as it was to them that I
couldn't make a living at it.

More than anything else I wanted to be an illustrator
like Norman Rockwell or Pruett Carter and paint pictures,
as they did, to accompany stories in magazines like the *La-*

dies' Home Journal, Good Housekeeping, and *Saturday Evening Post.*
My scholarship at art school did not provide enough money,
so I rather reluctantly went to work as a sketch artist in the
men's wardrobe department at 20th Century–Fox film studios.

Because I could draw like an illustrator, I was able to
present my proposals for wardrobe in vivid action sketches
which would usually carry the likeness of the actor who
would wear them in the film. Before long I was given designer status with an office-studio of my own. Hollywood
was at its zenith. Film budgets seemed to be limitless, film
stars were accorded the importance of royalty, and even
those of us who were merely servants in their courts gave
ourselves extravagant airs.

Self-indulgence was the order of the day. Dene's and
my interest in wine was pursued as far as we could take it.
Our small self-appointed cognoscenti spurned the local California wines, perhaps justifiably at that time, since the great
entrepreneurs of today's West Coast wine world had not yet
appeared and the general quality of that region's wine was
far below today's standards.

Dene was the most intoxicating thing in my life, however, and romance quickly fermented toward marriage. At
first we resisted such an important step. Hollywood might
take such things lightly, but our roots were in a more conservative world. We knew there were inevitable career
changes ahead for me and we were very young.

As it did for so many others, Pearl Harbor made the
decision for us. Against the ominous background of im-
pending war, long-term planning seemed silly. We drove to
Las Vegas one evening with a few friends and were married
in a quiet little chapel.

The World War II years interrupted our hedonistic education, but when they were over we returned to California
to resume the life we had enjoyed before. With the help of
my brother Sam, I built a house on a hilltop near Los Angeles, overlooking the San Fernando Valley. We became

interested in sports cars, through which we met another group of stimulating people. We drank wine with them, talked wine with them. We read books about wine. Wine had a daily place on our table. We even began to think about making our own wine. In fact, our constant talk of wine prompted a neighbor to suggest that we write to the State Agricultural College for advice on how to plant the hillside outside of our house with vines. It seemed a natural idea and I decided to do it.

But that's not what happened. When I returned to Fox after the war, the film industry was in the throes of incipient unionization. As a designer, I was of no interest to the union organizers; there were only a handful of us working in the entire industry at any one time. But, when Fox became embroiled in a particularly bitter interunion struggle involving my old artist chums, I decided to take a vacation rather than cross their picket lines. As the strike dragged on I had to find other work and turned to illustration to make a living.

An opportunity arose to go to New York, the center of the greatest market for magazine illustrators, and we bought a home in the suburban town of Hartsdale, forty-five minutes by train from New York City. I commuted by train to the city every day to work in advertising and at night continued to improve my skills as an illustrator.

The move east did not quell my interest in wine. Dene gave me a book, *The Wine Grower's Guide* by Philip Wagner, which triggered anew my desire to grow grapes. I ordered ten vines from Wagner's Boordy Vineyards nursery: Ravat 262 for red wines because it was a hybrid of Pinot Noir, a fine Burgundy grape, and l'Aurore, because it was described as very hardy. I planted them around the border of our half-acre garden, spacing them ten or more feet apart to assure plenty of sunlight on all the leaves. In no time they began to take over the garden—the shrubbery was overwhelmed. Dene even accused me of pulling out her peonies to make more room for vines.

Inside the house, things weren't much different. Because there was no attic or basement in the house there was little place to store things. I had begun to make wine, learning from Wagner's book how to test the grape juice for its sugar content with a saccharometer to determine the amount of alcohol that would be in the finished wine and how to find the acidity of the juice by using strips of litmus paper as an indicator. Since I needed more than I could grow, and there were no local sources of grapes, I bought grapes shipped from California to eastern produce markets for the express purpose of supplying home winemakers. The grapes, which were usually of the varieties Alicante Bouschet, Carignane, and sometimes Zinfandel for red wines and Thompson Seedless or Muscat for white wines, usually arrived around Columbus Day and were sold directly from the refrigerated freight car which had transported them.

I hadn't found a source for a barrel, which Wagner recommended as a fermenter, so I borrowed a large twenty-gallon crock from a neighbor whose German mother used it at other times for making sauerkraut. My two sons, aged three and five, were hardly taller than the walls of the crock and I still carry a vivid picture in my memory of the two of them inside the crock enthusiastically "squashing" the grapes with their feet.

At first we could only find a place for one or two five-gallon glass jars, or carboys, into which I put the juice from the squashed grapes to finish its fermentation. Soon the clothes closets were full of wine jugs. We kept our shoes under the bed because the floor space in the closet was filled with carboys. Even the fireplace was used to store wine. Inevitably some got spilled on the new carpet.

I became fascinated with finding and buying equipment for my new hobby. In my spare time, I'd often go to Spring or Mulberry street in New York City searching among the shops for a new press, an antique this or that. The family car was displaced and sat exposed to the weather in the driveway so the garage could shelter wine equipment. I still remember the look of disbelief on Dene's face one night when I told her that that morning while riding on the train I had spied a beautiful old wine press and stacks of barrels in someone's backyard. "I've got to go find them," I told her.

Finally, in exasperation I think, Dene said, "Mark, you've just got to have a farm." She had seen an advertisement in *Town and Country* magazine that described a small farm in Virginia. "Just the place for us," she thought—a place for cows, a vegetable garden, a stream and, of course, plenty of room for grapevines and wine jugs.

I began to get commissions to paint illustrations for stories in what we called household service magazines such as *McCall's, Good Housekeeping, Saturday Evening Post,* and so on. This was the goal I had been striving hard for, and once the breakthrough was achieved, I seemed to have what it took to succeed. My timing was bad, however. Television was taking hold in American society, and its enormous growth, together with the increasing use of photography in place of drawings and paintings were making such an impact on American advertising that three major magazines promptly went out of business. Household magazines curtailed their use of fiction and began to print more feature articles, many of these of the sort which could be more suitably and economically illustrated by photography.

In Europe, however, television and the use of photography had not yet become so common. The magazines were still providing light romantic fiction to receptive readers, and their editors were said to be willing to pay quite well to obtain illustrations from sound American artists. I gathered up a few typical samples of my work and flew to Paris to see what kind of a market I could find for my services.

Happily my reception in the offices of European publishers was more cordial than I could have imagined, and in both London and Paris, though I had made no advance appointments, I was given the most gracious welcome and a promise of future work.

A highlight of my visit to Paris was treating myself to

a dinner in a "great" restaurant, one of those *ne plus ultra* temples of dining which, like great wines, are so usually associated with France. On a rather whimsical basis I chose the Tour d'Argent restaurant because of its magnificent view of the historic Cathedral of Notre Dame, which is illuminated with floodlights in the evening.

When I arrived I sensed from a general air of excitement that something unusual was going on, but I did not notice anything in particular as I was led to a small table in the very middle of the dining room's center aisle beneath a large brightly lit chandelier. I felt as conspicuous as an actor on stage front and center. Nevertheless I was soon enjoying one of the establishment's most famous specialties, pressed duck, and sampling its excellent wines, and in spite of being alone I was having a grand time.

I had forgotten the earlier sense of excitement I had felt, when there was a sudden hush in the conversations about me. I glanced up. Every staff member of the restaurant seemed to have come to attention, their eyes all focused upon something behind me. I turned to look just in time to see the ex-President of the United States, Harry Truman, briskly leading a party of friends out of an alcove in the rear of the restaurant. There was a polite spattering of applause as he passed through the room. Since my table was directly in his path I felt compelled to stand, and as he passed I said, "Goodnight, Mr. President." Instantly, with the conditioned reflex of an old political campaigner, his hand reached out and warmly shook my own. "Goodnight, young man," he said. "I'm glad to see you."

When his party had passed I resumed my dinner, a little flustered and conscious of the fact that the President's ebulliently friendly gesture had called considerable attention to me. Apparently it had also given me a certain increase in status as well. My waiter seemed to be slightly more formal when he accompanied the cheese cart to my table. The sommelier approached to pour the bottle of Clos de Vougeot which had been opened earlier, and with him, the maître d'hotel. He waited until the sommelier had assured himself that I was pleased with the wine, then he said, "Would Monsieur care to visit our wine cellar after his cheese and have cognac and coffee in the tasting room?" I was delighted. It was the perfect way to finish an unusual evening.

Presently we descended by elevator to the *rez-de-chaussée,* then down a stone stairway to the enormous *cave,* where I was shown their rich store of great vintages. Many celebrities who regularly frequented the restaurant had their own private bins for storage of wines chosen and reserved for them alone. The bin of the Duke and Duchess of Windsor was pointed out in particular. After a brief tour we retired to a small cozy room adjacent to the cellars, where coffee and fine cognac were served in front of a fireplace. It was a rare privilege to visit the sanctum sanctorum in this historic old hostelry. As we sat and looked into the embers of the fire, I thought of the many famous names associated with its early history—Henri III, Madame de Sévigné, Alexandre Dumas—and silently I drank a toast to Harry Truman.

After I finished my business in Paris I decided to indulge myself in an overnight side trip to the wine country of Burgundy. To most people the little city of Beaune is the heart of Burgundy. It lies in the geographical center of the Côte d'Or, and even though it shares its commercial importance with Nuits-St.-Georges on the northern end of the Côte, its medieval charm has made it the destination of every tourist who wishes to visit Burgundy. It couldn't be reached directly by air but my guidebook told me that two of the fastest trains in western Europe, the Bleu Rapide and the Mistral, pass through it every day on their way to the French Riviera, whistling down through the center of France like the famous winds for which the morning train is named. I would have to *descendez* at Dijon, a few kilometers north, and bus the rest of the way. Nonetheless, my maps showed the bus route passing through vineyard lands. I asked my hotel concierge to reserve a ticket to Dijon for me on the Mistral so that I would have a chance to see more of the landscape in daylight. This was my first opportunity to get outside of city environments in any of the countries I had visited and I was very eager to see what it was like.

The French landscape as seen from the train seemed very intimate to me. Nearly every inch of it was in use. In the villages close to the city, every house seemed to have a kitchen garden. Fields were small, as if intended for private use rather than large-scale production. Instead of the ubiquitous two-car garage and extensive lawns of the American suburban scene, outbuildings were designed for the confinement and protection of farm animals. Cows grazed in nearly every yard, and a leggy rooster on the roof was not just a weather-vane decoration but an actual feather-bearing, crowing reality. As we moved south, fields grew somewhat larger and there was evidence of farming on a commercial scale. Still, the intimacy of the landscape persisted. There was almost no point on the journey when one could not see three or four little villages silhouetted on the horizon. Distances between them were short and reflected the fact that local transportation was by bicycle and shanks' mare rather than by fast modern vehicles. A few grapevines were growing in every garden but vineyards on any large scale were not to be seen.

We arrived at Dijon in about three hours' time. I found a taxi and drove to the bus station, where I made direct connections for the remainder of my trip, which was to terminate in Beaune. Leaving Dijon, the bus took the National Highway 74 to the south. From the point of view of my special interest there was nothing to be seen for quite a distance. A few fields of mustard, some black currants, but no grapevines. At last we passed a sign which brought me to rapt attention—"Fixin"—it said, and pointed to the right. Sure enough there in the distance were the unmistakable parallel rows of green I had come to see.

From here on the famous vineyard names appeared

regularly as the bus rushed along past signs marking the turn for Gevrey-Chambertin, Morey-St.-Denis, Chambolle-Musigny. By this time the vineyards were growing right up to the highway, the beautifully kept rows deep green against red stony soil. I was fairly hypnotized as they flashed past. Suddenly, the sight of a man in beret and blue clothes, riding an *enjambeur* tractor, which straddled the low trellised rows instead of running between them, made me remember my camera. I must have taken three thirty-six-exposure rolls

of film during the next fifteen minutes. Every village sign, every change of terrain, any sign of activity in the vineyards was snapped. Other passengers in the bus, used to the familiar scenery, must have thought me a strange one to spend my film so wildly on a landscape which was all so much the same.

The first really identifiable "postcard" scene we passed was the famous old Clos de Vougeot, sitting low among its vines about halfway up the slope. The *Clos*, or walled vineyards, were established by the Cistercian monks in the twelfth century. They reshaped and drained its swampy lowlands to create the largest of the really great plantations in Burgundy. Every few feet of its highway frontage there was an arched gateway bearing the name of an owner of a portion of its fabled vines.

The bus swept on past Vosne-Romanée into Nuits-St.-Georges, the capital of the Côte de Nuits and center of trade for the firm, full-textured, deep-colored wines of this northerly part of the "Golden Slope." Prémeaux was next, marking the southernmost limit of grape production in the Côte de Nuits. The Côte de Beaune begins with the vineyards of Pernand Vergelesses, just south of the village of Comblanchien, which is devoted to the quarrying of limestone, and continues through beautiful little Aloxe-Corton and Savigny-lès-Beaune, on into Beaune itself, then southward to include Pommard, Volnay, Meursault, Auxey-Duresses, Blagny, Puligny, Chassagne-Montrachet, and Santenay.

My brief stay in Beaune, which was so much more beautiful than I had expected, was spent wandering the narrow, cobblestoned streets of the inner city and admiring its curious mixture of architectural styles. I remember it gave the impression of bustling prosperity and friendliness, and I fell in love with it immediately. With only limited time I was able to see just a few of the city's surrounding vineyards, but by the end of the next day, when I began the journey home, I knew I had had my first glimpse of paradise.

On my return to New York we began to search quite seriously for a farm. Having grown up in small Oklahoma towns only about fifteen miles apart, Dene and I had lived in agricultural communities, had been raised among people who grew things, harvested them, and sold them. Owning a farm didn't seem to be an unusual thing. And, of course, we didn't think of grapes as being a big crop like cotton or cattle. We thought we were taking up a hobby. At the time we never dreamed that a vineyard farm would become the central focus of our lives. In fact, I think that is the difference from the people who come to call on us now. They have, in many cases, come to the point where they wish to break away from their professions and have a second career, whereas it was strictly an avocational interest with us. We didn't really think of it as anything else.

Since neither of us had any preconceived ideas as to the "only" place to search for our vineyard site, we drove out every weekend in a different direction looking for grape land. It was surprising how many places we found that had some historical association with viticulture. Whenever we described our needs to a local real-estate agent, he or she immediately thought of a property where "that old Frenchman used to have a couple of vines," or "Grandmother used to find wild grapes when she was a girl."

At one time we concentrated our search in Maryland because of our admiration for Philip Wagner and his work at the Boordy Vineyard in Riderwood there. But despite several trips to that area we were not able to find a suitable place.

Another trip to France and a three-month tour of the wine-growing region there opened our eyes to the potential of other areas in which grapes could be grown successfully. We roamed vineyards, from the Rhine to the Adriatic, tramping the rows, talking to the growers, examining their equipment, eating the local foods and drinking the local wines, gradually becoming more and more deeply enthusiastic. At any rate, I did.

By the time our summer was over I was almost obsessed with the idea of finding a place to plant vines, and as soon as we got back to America we took up our search again. We had returned rather low in funds, though, which made us remember that it was necessary for me to be near important commercial centers where there was a market for the work of an artist.

From the dozens of books I had read on the subject of grape growing, I learned that the mid-Hudson Valley was once a center of a burgeoning grape industry, so we made a few sorties up the river. It seemed to have the right sort of land—there were actually grapes to be seen as we drove along the roads.

The sight of growing vines was as exciting to me as a red flag to a bull. No matter that the varieties growing were probably juice and jelly grapes, unsuitable for winemaking, I intended to plant my own choice of vines. The mere presence of sizable vineyards of any sort said that here was the probability of a climate of adequate rainfall, at least a minimal growing season, and tolerable winter temperatures. As the leaves fell and the terrain became exposed we could see that nearly every hillside had once borne grapes, even those now overgrown with weeds and brush. The gaunt landscape was ribbed with narrow horse-plowed terraces. The woods were hung with great swinging vines. To a grape grower (and already I thought of myself as one) these wooded areas were filled with the history of a vigorous grape industry long since passed.

The trees, sometimes more than thirty feet tall, all grew in orderly ranks, marking old vineyard rows, where their roots, chopped back during the days when vines were being cultivated, had lain in wait. Then, when the vineyard was abandoned, they had leapt toward the sky, benefiting from the fertilization and tillage that had been given the soil in past years. In most cases the vines had expired from lack of pruning and lack of sunlight, shaded by the vigorous young trees. But occasionally an intrepid vine would refuse to give up, its tendrils clutching one low branch to reach a higher one until at last it reached the treetop, where it spread its canes among the branches, insisting upon its fair share of sun and fresh air. These vines developed again a kind of wild wisdom, which kept them from trying to produce too much fruit from their copious branches as a domestic vine will do, to its great damage, if not pruned carefully by its vineyard manager. In the years since, I have come across vines in my own woods forty feet or more in length, carrying their life-giving fluids through multiple trunks four inches in diameter from a base almost three feet across.

These woods were like an old battlefield, the ghost of past struggles were all around, and although I didn't realize it then those gaunt surviving vines reaching silently toward the light also symbolized the glorious, comic, sometimes nearly tragic struggle I was about to enter. Drawn by an indescribable scent of adventure which rises, for some people, from the dark, fragrant, ruby-glinting depths of this ancient liquid, I was about to commit the remaining years of my life to the production of wine.

Somewhere in a book I had seen a striking photograph of a fine old Hudson Valley vineyard planted in what appeared to be a steadily ascending terrace winding from the base of a moundlike hill, around and upward to its top, where there stood a simple wooden cross. "The Vineyard at Christian Hill," the caption read without mentioning its location. One rainy day as Dene and I were driving along Route 9W, I glanced toward the river and there, silhouetted against the squally sky, was Christian Hill!

It was bare now, its vines long since dead, its winding terraces barely discernible through the brush grown over them. Its old cross was still standing, and in the dim light of this stormy afternoon one could imagine the vineyard in its prime. I stopped the car for a few moments to gaze at this relic from other days. Having done so I became aware of other features of the surrounding landscape which otherwise I might have missed, since our goal for the afternoon's drive was further up the road, where we had an appointment to look at some property. Near the base of Christian Hill was a fine old-fashioned barn with shuttered windows, a large arched doorway, and an ornate Victorian cupola topped by a weather vane. A few hundred yards to the south a pretty little red brick church stood under its ancient elms, against the background of the river. As we drove on into a small village I was pleased by a large old frame house with a little barn, both neatly maintained and freshly painted.

This was my first impression of the town of Marlboro, which was to figure so largely in the next years of my life. I liked it. We went on our way that day to keep our appointment. We frequently went through the village in the follow-

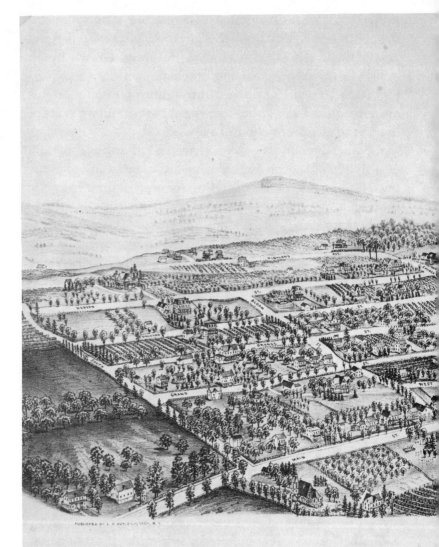

PUBLISHED BY L. R. BURLEIGH, TROY, N. Y.

1 M. E. Church.
2 Presbyterian Church.
3 Roman Catholic Church.
4 Episcopal Church.
5 Public School.
6 Woolen Mill, Sheard & Gibson, Props.
7 Fruit Crate Factory, D. W. Kniffin, Prop.
8 Charles Warren, General Merchandise.

   Emmet Warren, Meat Market.
9 C. H. Harris, General Bakery & Ice Cream Rooms
10 Office of David Mosher, Physician & Surgeon.
11 Wm. H. Newman, Plumbing, Stove & Tin Store.
12 Exchange Hotel, Henry M. Kniffin, Prop.
13 C. H. Kniffin, General Store & Post Office.
14 J. C. Merritt, General Merchandise.
15 John Badner, Meat Market & General Store.

MARLBO

GH, N. Y.

16 S. F. Burgess, Furniture, Carpets & Oil Cloth.
17 Office of A. H. Palmer, Physician & Surgeon.
18 Philip A. Rion, Funeral Director.
19 E. E. McNamee, Druggist & Chemist.
20 A. B. Masten, House & Carriage Painting.
21 M. V. B. Morgan, Meat Market.
22 J. S. Carpenter, General Merchandise.
23 Samuel Corwin's Sons, Hardware & Groceries.

24 Samuel Corwin's Sons, Dry Goods.
25 Pleasant View Hotel, M. McMullen.
26 Ne W. Wright's Sons, Flour, Feed and General
     Grist Mill.
27 Marlborough Record Office, E. E. Carr,
     Editor and Prop.
28 Lawson Taylor, Blacksmithing.
29 Whitney Basket Co's Manufactory

ing weeks, on our way to see properties for sale. Subsequent impressions, however, without the dramatic sky and the surprise view of old Christian Hill to fire the imagination, were somewhat less favorable. Marlboro was really just an old rundown fruit town. Like the vineyards overrun by woods, it was a relic of a past, more prosperous time. Its main street was not paved. Its few stores were, for the most part, not neatly kept. No one seemed to take pride in them any more, even though the old buildings were interesting in shape and could have looked very nice indeed with a coat of paint and a flower or two here and there to set them off. Nonetheless, Marlboro began to be a kind of center for our explorations. It was, after all, a real fruit growers' town in a region which still produced vine, tree, and bush fruits as its major economic interest. In such an environment I would be likely to find the services, the trained help, and experienced advice I would probably need to carry out my own plans. A check with the county agent about early and late frost dates, minimum winter temperatures, and so on—factors that all prospective winegrowers should look into before they invest in the land they hope to cultivate—indicated almost perfect conditions for our purposes. With all its aesthetic shortcomings, Marlboro was grape country.

From many conversations with real-estate brokers and chance acquaintances and from reading, I learned interesting historical details about the town. In its past it had been a major center for grape experimentation and cultivation, part of a region which U. P. Hedrick, author of the *Grapes of New York,* referred to as "the birthplace of American viticulture." The grape and wine industry of the United States was started in this valley. Outstanding viticulturists such as J. H. Ricketts, W. D. Barnes, Dr. C. W. Grant, and Dr. W. M. Culbert had lived and done their work within a few miles. These men had done more than grow and sell grapes. They had accumulated practical knowledge and trained the men who spread this knowledge through our nation. One of the most respected of these great pioneer viticulturists, A. J.

Caywood, had actually lived in this very town. From his vineyards had come some of the finest of the early American hybrid vines, including the famous Dutchess grape, which is still regarded as the best wine grape to have its origins in eastern America. Somewhere around here there must be a place which could serve our purpose. We were homing in on our quest.

When I came upon Benmarl, my real-estate agent, a wise lady who after a few meetings had seen immediately to the heart of my interests, wasted little time on the two houses, barn and tumbledown outbuildings, none of which had seen a coat of paint in twenty-five years. As she speedily trotted me around the house that was to serve as a residence, she talked only of the vineyards, "one of the oldest and finest vineyards in the state," she said, "established in the 1800s." The owner, Mr. William Wardell, took her hint and quickly suggested a tour of the "upper vineyards," where his grandfather, "Mr. Caywood," had carried on his experiments. I was startled by the mention of this man whom I had so recently read about. Until that moment I had not been greatly impressed with the property. In spite of my good agent's avoidance of the condition of the farm, I had seen what a great deal of work it would require to make it a comfortable place in which to live. Now I could barely contain my excitement and impatience to see the rest of it.

We set out in the owner's dilapidated old Model-T Ford

along an incredibly steep narrow road, which had been carved out of the hillside by a horse and plow and certainly was never meant for an automobile, even the rugged Model-T. We cut right along the old vineyard rows, bouncing on the rocks and dropping hard into the woodchuck holes. Once or twice he slowed to point at a row of thick-trunked old vines. "These are over a hundred years old," he said, or "Those vines, fourth from the end, are some of grandfather's experiments, Dutchess, I think."

Suddenly we came out onto a high shale plateau. He stopped the vehicle and invited me to step down. He took his walking stick and pushed aside some young sumac bushes at the edge of the bluff so that we could see the terraced ranks of the old vines dropping sharply toward the river, some four hundred feet below us. From this point there was no highway, no gas station, no factory, nor any other feature of the twentieth century to be seen, only the silent handsomely ordered patterns of orchards and vineyards carpeting the valley floor under the distant Connecticut hills. Except for the dilapidated state of the vines around us I might have been standing with Caywood himself, looking at the landscape as he saw it. To me it was breathtaking. Love at first sight. We stood there for a time without saying anything. I was spellbound. Finally, Mr. Wardell said, "Always thought I'd build a little shack up here to spend some time in during the summer," as if to suggest this as an inducement to me. He was too late to initiate the idea. In those few moments I had restored all the old vineyards and built a fine *château* in which to stand guard over them.

As I drove home later that afternoon, I began to rehearse my report of the day's exciting events to Dene, who had stayed home this weekend. Somehow, though, no matter how I described the farm I had fallen in love with, it always sounded like a big responsibility, which would require a great deal of time and money to convert into a comfortable country place. The house we would use for a residence possessed enormous shortcomings; no indoor water supply, an ancient coal furnace, a coal-burning kitchen stove, limited electricity—the list was endless. As an artist, I was fascinated by the sense of frozen time I had felt during the whole visit, by the hundred of paintable scenes both inside and outside the house.

But I knew my practical wife would point out that it wasn't necessary to buy a landscape in order to paint it. What we were looking for was a *small* piece of land on which to plant a *few* vines, with a *comfortable* little summer house. We both had busy, demanding lives. We needed a place to escape to on weekends where we could, by diverting our energies to tending a little vineyard and perhaps a vegetable garden, soothe our frayed nerves, refresh our enthusiasm for plunging back into our real lives on Monday morning.

The following Saturday I drove Dene up to see "my farm." She knew it was my farm, I think, before we made the trip. I had tried to be fair in my description of the place. No unpleasant details had been left out. But she heard something else between the lines as I talked which warned her that as far as I was concerned we had come to the end of the search. My second visit didn't improve the appearance of things. Even though I had chosen a bright and sunny day to introduce it to my wife, there was no way to minimize the difference between this rundown old farm and her shining dream of a country place. Dene was brave. A few feeble arguments against it, perhaps a tear or two were shed, but in the end she gamely agreed that we would find a way to make it do. "Don't worry," I said. "It's a working farm! It will pay for itself. Anyway, it's only a summer place. I promise, you'll never have to live there."

So we bought it. Dene started planning the renovation of the house and I began preparing to plant vines, learning the difference between a book *vigneron* and a real one. There was a lot to learn.

chapter II

The Initiation

We became the owners of Benmarl in September 1957, just
after the last of the Delaware grapes had been picked. As
soon as I knew that there was finally a place to plant them
I began to consider just which of the many varieties of wine
grapes available would be the best to start with. We had no
local precedent to help us decide. Even though there were a
number of flourishing vineyards in our area, only the Concord, Niagara, some Catawba, and a few Delaware vines
were grown in them. In terms of our specialized interest in
producing fine table wines in the European style these were
not really wine grapes because their flavor is too assertive,
without the subtlety of good wine grapes. Our interests lay
in varieties that were already known to produce excellent
wines in the old-world wine regions, the fabled viniferas

that I had tasted and read about since I had first become interested in wine, and the exciting, relatively new French hybrids that I had read about in Philip Wagner's books. When we mentioned planting European grapes the old-timers in the town shook their heads—no one had tried anything as foolish as that in over a hundred years, except perhaps someone from the old country who had sneaked in a vine or two with him on the boat, "and all those had died within a short time or gone wild again and lost their European flavor."

Everett Crosby's High Tor Vineyards, forty miles to the south of us, provided the best opportunity to observe some of the varieties that interested us, with soil and climate conditions reasonably similar to our own. I visited Everett regularly and he was unfailingly cooperative and encouraging, making all of his considerable experience freely available to me. We both felt that the varieties that he was growing successfully, such as Baco Noir and Seibel 4986, would do equally well on my land. The wines he was making from them were very attractive; the whites in particular were fresh and delicious. He felt at that time that really big, hearty red wines were going to be more difficult to achieve. Nevertheless, his red wines were such an enormous improvement over any made previously in New York that they represented a real breakthrough toward the goal he and I were seeking. The precedent set by Crosby represents an important period in the viticultural history of the Hudson region. His success, which he wrote about in a delightful and instructive book, provided a necessary example of what could be done, and his bluff, hearty personality was a source of encouragement to many beginners, some of whom, like myself, have established vineyards and carried on his example in other regions.

As most of the eastern experimenters of this period did, I relied greatly on the books and advice of Philip Wagner to guide me on everything. His magnificent book, *The Wine*

Grower's Guide, provided the only American published text-book on eastern vineyard management and vine selection. Dene and I had visited him and his charming wife, Jocelyn, at their home in Riderwood, Maryland, during the early days of our search for vineyard land, and indeed it was his confirmation of the Hudson River region's suitability that prompted our first investigations of this area. Marlboro lies in District Number Two of Wagner's map of "The American Grape Growing Districts." This district includes all the principal present grape-growing sections in the United States outside of California. Its climate conditions are such that a great many of the vinifera varieties and French hybrids appeared likely to succeed in it.

Actually, Benmarl has an advantage over the rest of its neighboring fruit land in the way it lies relative to the path of the sun. The air and water drainage of its slopes gives it a highly favorable microclimate, which protects its early-budding vines from the early frosts. It collects more degree days of heat during the summer months and extends the ripening season somewhat longer than normal for this area. This advantage was more or less a theoretical one to me at that time, however, for although both Mr. Wardell, the previous owner, and his hired man assured me that I would be able to grow more delicate grapes than others around me, none of us could guess to what extent we could press this advantage. I decided to hedge the decisions by planting a few vines of nearly all the varieties that looked possible for my region, in a kind of experimental "garden vineyard," where I could watch their performance for a while before selecting those that would be worth expanding. Meantime, for more immediate use, we would select spots in the upper vineyard areas to be prepared for "nucleus" plantings of those varieties that we knew to be good wine producers and whose growing characteristics were most compatible with our climate. These nucleus vineyards were to be located some distance apart so that, assuming they did as well as expected, they could be expanded later on into two- or three-acre plots of the same variety. Relying on Wagner, Crosby, and some correspondence with Monsieur Pierre Galet, whom I had met when he was the Chef de Viticulture at the École Nationale d'Agriculture at Montpellier, France, and who knew more about Benmarl's weather conditions than any of my advisors who lived in the Hudson Valley, and a bit of guesswork, we ordered our first producers.

From Wagner's Boordy Vineyards nursery I selected for the nucleus vineyards French hybrid varieties Baco Noir, Maréchal Foch, Léon Millot, and Landot 244 for red wines, Seyval Blanc and l'Aurore for white wines. These were ordered in quantities of three hundred each, enough to comfortably produce barrel-sized vintages for our winemaking experiments. At the same time I ordered some sixty other varieties in quantities of five or six each from Wagner and the Canadian Experiment Station in Ontario. These were for the "garden vineyard." Successful ones could be expanded later. Fifty vines of various vinifera varieties including Chardonnay, Riesling, Sauvignon Blanc, Pinot Noir, and Zinfandel were ordered from California.

Once the decision was made and the vines ordered I was able to turn my attention to other things. There was plenty to do. Even though I had bought forty-odd acres of land, practically none of it was in condition to use for planting without a great deal of preparation. Sites for the new vines had to be selected, cleared, and plowed so the soil would be workable by spring. We were already into autumn. With so little to work with and so little experience of my own to draw on, the problem of getting ready for the arrival of something like fourteen hundred grapevines seemed an almost overwhelming task. Also, in addition to this, something had to be done about the old vines already producing grapes. Most of them were suffering from years of inadequate attention. Few of them, in fact, were worth the effort of rehabilitation. For some reason, Mr. Caywood's most famous hybrid, the Dutchess, was represented by only a few vines. The only surviving vineyards of any interest to me were those planted to the Delaware grape. This old variety is an especially attractive one for table use and is also considered one of the best of the so-called "classic" American varieties for winemaking. Since we were three or four years away from a vintage of the new grapes, the Delawares were essential to keep us afloat.

There was no tractor on the place. All tillage had been done by a horse pulling a gap-toothed spring harrow through the three-to-four-foot-wide rows, and weed control under the trellis was accomplished by an old black hired man, Milton Barnes, who guided a hand plow with marvelous skill along the base of the vines, first turning a furrow away from the vines, then a few weeks later throwing it back, covering up the weeds that had grown again. There was no working sprayer. Fungus and insect control was apparently managed by prayer alone. Milton did it all, both the plowing and the praying.

I sensed Milton was worried about whether or not he would be allowed to stay on after we took over the farm, and so was I. Although he seemed to know grapes very well, I wondered if he could adapt to modern farming methods. Also, he was pretty old to launch into a vigorous new undertaking. It was difficult to tell just how old he was. He didn't look old, but he had been retired for many years from working on the railroad. He was very tall when he held himself erect, though normally he stood slightly bowed. He was quite handsome, with a very calm, dignified, kindly manner. He had injured a leg in earlier years working for the railroad and walked with a rather irregular, lopsided gait, almost as if he were intoxicated. The injury made it impossible for him to drive a tractor, although it didn't interfere with his ability to work in other ways.

I was impressed by the way he knew the terrain of the farm. Like many people in the area in those days he foraged

for a great deal of his food. He kept at least three dogs, which were trained to hunt, and they regularly ranged over the farm in all seasons in search of small game. He knew all the boundary lines. In fact, it was he rather than Mr. Wardell who walked the perimeter of the property to show me just what I had purchased. He seemed able to identify every variety of tree and plant. Even though much of the land had not been worked during his stay there he had a good idea of where the soil was deep or shaly or clay-bottomed, by the kind of plants that grew voluntarily in each area. He knew the frosty spots as well as the hill faces which warm up first in the spring. There was no doubt that he could be very helpful to me. My plans, though, were to convert the farm to machine cultivation, and I was afraid that his inability to operate a tractor would outweigh his other talents. A younger man should probably occupy his cottage. Nonetheless, I agreed that he should stay, at least through the winter. Then we would "see how things develop." As it turned out, keeping Milton was the luckiest thing that ever happened. He became my very close friend and advisor. Without him I'm not sure I would have gotten through the first years.

I bought a good used Ferguson tractor with a new engine and a few attachments, depending largely on Milton's advice as to which ones would be most useful. His advice was always freely given when asked for, but rarely proffered until then. I learned to ask for it. Once, after a hard afternoon's work with a post-hole digger of the hand type with two digging blades and two long handles, I made up my mind to buy a tractor auger to use for setting trellis posts. I didn't mention my plans to Milton, and when I proudly brought out my new tool the following weekend he was politely congratulatory and went on about his work. Before I finished drilling the second hole I began to suspect I had made a mistake. The soil of Benmarl is extremely stony, and although the auger could cope with a lot, whenever the tip came down squarely on a stone in its path, it was unable to do anything more than spin helplessly until I dismounted and dug the obstruction out with a pick and shovel. My labor-saving device was certainly not a timesaver. After four hours' work I had only five posts installed. Worse still, the posts were not really secure in the oversized augered holes. Belatedly, I went to get Milton's advice.

I followed him over to the tool shed, where he rummaged around until he found an iron bar about five feet long with a small football-shaped swelling on one end. We went over to the scene of my frustrated labors. Choosing the next post site, he began to dig by lifting the bar and driving the point of the swollen end into the rocky earth. After each down stroke, he pulled the top of the bar around in a wide circular motion. This widened the hole and packed the dirt around it. The bar seemed almost to drop through the ground, simply pushing aside any stones it met, packing them into the sides of the hole. After a couple of dozen strokes he had made a neat hole about two and a half feet deep and just a fraction smaller than a grape post. He then placed the pointed end of a post into his excavation and drove it home with a sledgehammer. In less than a quarter of my best time there stood a post as securely packed into the ground as if it had been set in concrete. He called the bar a "podger." For our type of land it is an amazing tool. If there is a place where you couldn't set a post with the podger you simply would have to dynamite.

The major problem in the rehabilitation of the old Delaware vineyards was that they had been planted for horse cultivation, in rows only about four feet apart. The first thing we had to do was to remove every other row in order to get our tractor through. On flat ground there was no difficulty. We just pulled up the posts, cut off the vines, and harrowed out the roots. Very little of our land, however, is flat, and when we approached the terraced vineyards on the side hills we ran into insurmountable problems. If we took out a row, there was a shelf left running right down the center of our tractor path. The corridor between trellises was too narrow to allow a bulldozer to reterrace it, and after a few precarious passes through with our tractor on a forty-five-degree angle I had to abandon the hope of saving these vines for even temporary use. Luckily there proved to be enough viable vines on manageable land to keep us from dying of thirst.

After the Delaware rows were widened and their trellises shored up enough to face another year, we turned to the selection and preparation of sites for the experimental "garden" vineyard, where we could put ten each of about fifty varieties for observation, and six nucleus vineyards, which were to be the first of our real wine-grape producers. There was very little time left before cold weather would put an end to our outside work for the season. I was lucky enough to find a bulldozer operator with a machine large enough to clear a five-acre block of old vineyard land that had not been used for what Mr. Wardell reckoned was at least twenty-five years. The trees in it were twenty to thirty feet tall and grew as thick as hedges. When the job was done, we had a beautiful field, undoubtedly better than it had been when used before because the big dozer had been able to tear off the shale outcroppings, fill in the low spots, and shape a softly rolling surface on the slope, which tilted perfectly to the southeasterly sky. We decided to reserve this new space to two varieties, Baco Noir and Seyval Blanc.

Actually, I made two mistakes during the clearing of this piece of land. One, I didn't clear enough of it while I was at it. A newly cleared area just wrested from the woods that stand around the edges of it always seems a good deal larger than it does later when it is laid out for planting. Later, when I got around to enlarging this vineyard, it was extremely tricky to fell the nearby trees without endangering the existing vines. Two, I left a tree to grow right in the middle of the clearing.

It was one of those situations that illustrates the special difficulties apt to be encountered by an artist turned farmer. I was riding on the bulldozer with the operator in order to show him how I wanted the land shaped when we came upon a nice little baby oak tree standing alone atop a shale outcropping. It was only about fifteen feet tall and so perfectly shaped that on impulse I directed the dozer away from it. As we cleared around it I could see that there was so much shale at its base that even if it was removed no vines could be planted on the barren ground. A short while later I glanced back at it and saw that my two sons, Kim and Eric, aged twelve and ten, had climbed into its bare branches and were happily observing the proceedings, like two merry little birds.

The analogy I had instinctively made to birds should have warned me then but it didn't. I only saw that two happy youngsters had adopted a tree I hadn't wanted to destroy, saving it "to give a little contrast to the landscape." Within two seasons, the little tree, freed of all competition, had doubled in size. Now it has crowded out enough nearby trellis space to accommodate ten or more vines, and during the summer it serves as a refuge for families of birds, which prey on the ripening grapes. I frequently chide myself for the sentimental impulse that made me leave the tree, but on the other hand I find equally frequently that, when I'm working in that part of the farm on a hot day, I find an excuse to take a break and sit for a while under its wide, spreading branches. As I relax in its shade and look out upon the fine view of the valley that its rocky knoll commands, I'm reminded that there is room for us all—the tree, my wine vines, and even the birds that will soon begin to take their pay for the cheerful concert they have provided all year.

Seibel 5279, also known as "l'Aurore," is one of the older of the French hybrids, widely known throughout Europe for its hardiness and dependability. I decided to give it one of the fairly flat, easy-to-work sites, which had recently been used for growing vegetables and was therefore in excellent shape for planting. If all else failed, I reasoned, we would have some Aurore as our *vignes de sécurité*. Later it was removed after other varieties proved to be more to our taste.

Maréchal Foch, as well as Landot 244, both red-wine producers, were assigned plots that had recently been used as vineyards. These, I realized, were not ideal site selections. The land should have been turned over a few times and planted with some sort of cereal for a few seasons to put it in the best condition for reuse. We just didn't have time to wait. Neither of these two vineyards developed as they would have with properly prepared sites. Foch recovered well and grew satisfactorily after a slow first and second season. Landot 244 had to be removed. Its former location was eventually completely rebuilt by the addition of tons of topsoil and used as a nursery for the rooting of cuttings for our vineyard expansion.

Chardonnay is regarded as a cold-sensitive variety. We decided to prepare a well-protected side-hill location with especially good air drainage for it. This meant carving terraces into the slope so that the tractor would be able to travel on a safe flat path across its face. Many of the older vineyards in the Marlboro area were planted in rows which ran up and down the hills rather than across them. The loss of topsoil due to erosion was naturally very heavy on steep sites. I had frequently wondered why the old planters had laid out their vineyards in this manner, which so obviously robbed the land of its vitality.

As I worked with my own land I discovered the reason. Most of the land that lies along the banks of the Hudson River in this region is underlaid with great sheets of slate, which, without going deeply into its geological history, was probably deposited by the sea in the early Mesozoic era. The sea receded; then, during the last glacial period, which covered the Northeast and created the Hudson River, these sheet deposits were crumpled and uplifted, and left in rows, tilted on edge, usually parallel to the river. Gradually the spaces between them were filled in over the centuries with clay, sand, and gravel and at last a thin layer of topsoil. Their jagged edges, where they break through the surface, are a familiar feature of the valley landscape and thousands more of them lie just under the ground to snag a plow or harrow when a farmer attempts to work a row or furrow laid out across them. Since the early vineyardists didn't have the giant earth-moving machines available today to remove these obstacles, they found it necessary to plant between the up-ended sheets of rock, accepting the tilt of the terrain however it ran.

Fortunately, the site we had chosen for Chardonnay was arranged in such a way that our terraces could run along the slope face without crossing an outcropping. Even though our tools would frequently encounter an edge of it, they could slide along the grain of the rock without hanging up. We were able to build this vineyard ourselves with our own tractor and an attachment aptly called a blade terracer. This blade, pulled behind the machine, can be adjusted to any desired tilt and cutting angle in much the way that a snow plow can. By cutting into the earth on its leading edge and moving it across and depositing it on its trailing edge the tool, in the hands of a patient operator, can build as fine a terrace as any bulldozer, if no large stones get in the way. Milton and I worked as a team. Wherever I encountered a stone too large to pull up with the blade he would dig until we could wrap a heavy chain around it and drag it out of our path with the tractor. We worked well into December on our task. Long after most of the earth on other parts of the farm was frozen hard, this sheltered sunny spot was mild and its soil soft. Finally, shortly before Christmas, on a brisk afternoon we came to the end of our labors.

The day had started bright but became increasingly cloudy during the afternoon. As a wind began to move down from the north we watched snow squalls slide along the river. It was an astonishing sight from our high position. We could see over and around the ends of each miniature storm as it scooted along just above the surface of the water, depositing a light powdering of white on the trees along the bank. Then I began to feel the tractor labor as it dragged the blade over what appeared to be soft, loose dirt. The soil was jelling. Within an hour it was rock hard. Winter had arrived. The rest of the job would have to wait until spring.

chapter III

A Backward Glance

In the short two months during the winter before pruning and the actual planting of vineyards could begin, our little project underwent a subtle change. There was time to study the early history of our newly adopted area. Hours spent in conversation with Mr. Wardell and Mrs. Edith Caywood Meckes, Andrew Caywood's granddaughter, transformed their memories of early days into a romantic picture, at least in my mind, of a specially destined grape farm which, through a series of unfortunate flukes, had never realized its true potential. The more we learned of early Marlborough, as it was originally spelled, and the Caywood legend the more we felt that his work, had it been pursued, *could* have made the mid-Hudson area a major wine-producing region.

The "science" of agriculture, as we think of it today,

had not yet emerged when Caywood first planted Benmarl. Viniculture, that is the cultivation of grapes for winemaking, although one of man's oldest pursuits, was hardly more than a folk art based upon centuries of empirical observation by European *vignerons*. Pasteur had not yet discovered the secret of biological fermentation. When colonists tried to grow wine grapes in the new world of America this folk science failed. Everyone was baffled by the fact that wine grapes brought to America from Europe succumbed within a few years to various unfamiliar and uncontrollable maladies. This was mysterious because the new world was liberally endowed with native grapevines, which were apparently thriving. Unfortunately, wine made from these wild grapes was not considered to be of acceptable quality because of its strong, unsubtle flavor and aroma. The cause of the failure of the European grapes, when transplanted here, was eventually discovered to be a combination of hazards: a tiny insect, which eventually became known as "phylloxera," as well as various fungus and virus diseases, all native to America and devastatingly damaging to the imported European wine grapes while being comparatively harmless to the wild native vines. The direct control of these pests would not even begin until 1894, when an American named C. V. Riley would identify phylloxera and invent the first agricultural sprayer.

In spite of these difficulties, however, during the early 1700s in the Hudson Valley a viticulture had developed on a modest scale among a colony of French Huguenots who had settled around the New Paltz area and had spread through much of the County of Ulster and south along the Hudson River. Old records indicate that a community known as New Marlborough-on-the-Hudson was successfully cultivating vines in 1782, and by 1788 it had become an incorporated village using a cluster of grapes as the decorative symbol of its town seal.

Further down the valley a doctor, Richard A. Underhill, had established a sizable vineyard in 1827 at Croton Point in Westchester County. Eventually it grew to some seventy-five acres and, as America's first commercial-scale vineyard, supplied grapes to the big city markets on both ends of the valley.

The reason for the success of the Huguenots and the subsequent spread of viticulture along the banks of the Hudson River lies at least partly in the soil and climate of this area. As I just mentioned, when America's commercial grape growing was born here the modern science of viticulture did not yet exist. Even spraying was unknown. There was very little that the grape grower anywhere in the world could do in the face of adversity but suffer and pray. However, here the relatively benign conditions of the region provided an environment more naturally suited to grape growing than any which had yet been tried in America.

The latitude of the mid-Hudson area corresponds to that of Rome in Italy, thus placing it in a zone which receives direct intense sunlight over a longer period of the year than the Rhineland of Germany or even the best vineyards of France. The Hudson winters, of course, are much more severe than those of Europe, owing to the tendency of cold Canadian air to swoop down upon the valley during the months of January and February, frequently lowering temperatures to below zero Fahrenheit. This hazard, however, has its compensations. A grape plant is, of course, dormant during this period, and because it has been well ripened in the long Hudson summer, it can endure this temperature without harm, and the deep winter cold serves as a kind of sanitizing period, discouraging the buildup of insect and fungus predators to which the area would otherwise be subject.

The microclimates of the Hudson Valley change as one moves along the river because of the diversity of its terrain and the wide variety of atmospheric influences to which it is subject. In the part of the valley where grapes are grown, the summer temperature is high, owing to its latitude and its position between ranges of mountains and to southerly winds which prevail during the growing season. (The period for ripening here is generally a week to fifteen days longer than in other New York vineyards.) The influence of the river, actually a broad estuary in the vine region, is at all seasons very favorable to grape growing. Although adequate amounts of rainfall are received in the Hudson vineyard region, excess is prevented here because moisture being carried inland from the Atlantic is largely precipitated by the mountains and highlands of New England. This also is very favorable to grape growing. In addition, the summer rain is principally in July, whereas other New York vineyard areas tend to experience heavy rains in September or October, making maturity and harvesting of the fruit more difficult.

Another great blessing is that the soils of the mid-Hudson grape lands are of the geologic division known as the Taconic Province, a broad valley extending from Pennsylvania across New Jersey, taking in parts of Ulster, Orange, Dutchess, and Columbia counties in New York. The rocks of this geologic division are shales, schists, and limestones. The soil is derived from them. The finer grape lands in this area are those in which there is much slate or shale in rather coarse fragments, such as is found on the Benmarl estate vineyards.

By the end of the Civil War, Hudson Valley grape growing was considered to be one of the nation's most promising industries. The papers of the time, *Frank Leslie's Illustrated Newspaper, Harper's Weekly,* and others, were filled with articles about Hudson Valley grape growing, copiously illustrated with drawings and engravings of vineyards and river boats being loaded with grapes for the distant markets. Among the young farmers attracted to the valley at the time, Andrew Caywood, who had married into the Underhill family, became interested in grape growing and purchased a vineyard of his own on an extremely rugged but beautiful hill property (now Benmarl) in the old town of Marlborough. Here he found himself in the company of other grape growers, whose curiosity about the ills besetting viti-

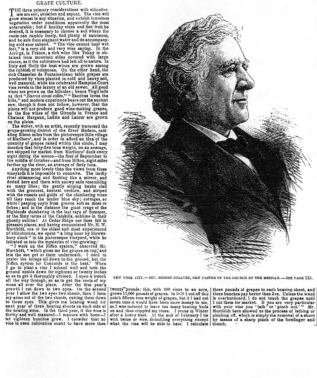

NEW YORK.—GROWING AMERICAN INDUSTRIES—TRIMMING AND PACKING GRAPES FOR MARKET, NEAR MARLBORO'-ON-THE-HUDSON.—FROM A SKETCH BY OUR SPECIAL ARTIST.

GRAPE CULTURE.

THE three primary considerations with viticulturists are soil, situation and aspect. The vine will grow almost in any situation, and exhibit luxurious vegetation under conditions apparently the most unfavorable; but if healthy vines and fine fruit be desired, it is necessary to choose a soil where the roots can ramble freely, find plenty of nutriment, and be safe from stagnant water and its accompanying cold sour subsoil. "The vine cannot bear wet feet," is a very old and very wise saying. In the Arriège, in France, a rich wine like Tokay is obtained from mountain sides covered with large stones, as it the cultivators had left all to nature. In Italy and Sicily the best wines are grown among the rubbish of volcanoes. On the other hand, the rich Chasselas de Fontainebleau table grapes are produced by vines planted in cold and heavy soil, well manured, while the celebrated Hampton Court vine revels in the luxury of an old sewer. All good vines are grown on the hillsides; hence Virgil tells us that "Bacchus amat colles," "Bacchus loves the hills," and modern experience bears out the ancient saw, though it does not follow, however, that the plains will not produce good wine-making grapes, as the fine wines of the Gironde in France and Chateau Margaux, Lafitte and Latour are grown on the plains.

The writer, with an artist, recently traversed the grape-growing district of the River Hudson, radiating fifteen miles from the picturesque little village of Marlboro', and in order to afford an idea of the quantity of grapes raised within this circle, I may mention that forty-five tons weight, on an average, are shipped for market from Marlboro' dock every night during the season—the first of September to the middle of October—and from Milton, eight miles further up the river, an average of forty tons.

Anything more lovely than the views from these vineyards it is impossible to conceive. The lordly river shimmering and flashing like a mirror, and dotted here and there with snowy sails resembling so many lilies; the gently sloping banks clad with the greenest, keenest verdure, and striped with the russets and golds of the clambering vines till they reach the tender blue sky; cottages, so white! peeping coyly from groves soft as moss or lichen; and in the distance the giant crags of the Highlands slumbering in the last rays of Summer, or the filmy forms of the Catskills, sublime in their ghostly outline! At Cedar Ridge our lines fell in pleasant places, and having encountered Mr. H. W. Murtfeldt, one of the oldest and most experienced of viticulturists, we spent "a long hour by Shrewsbury clock" in his picturesque vineyard, while he initiated us into the mysteries of vine-growing.

"I work on the Niffen system," observed Mr. Murtfeldt, "which gives me the grapes on top,' and lets the sun get at them underneath. I used to prefer the foliage all down to the ground, but the Niffen system for Concords is the best." When I go to plant a vine I subsoil well and turn the ground upside down for eighteen or twenty inches so as to get it thoroughly drained. I open a trench all the way through, so as to get the roots of my vines all over the place. After the first year's growth I cut down to two eyes. On the second year I allow the two eyes two shoots, then I form my arms out of the two shoots, cutting them down to three eyes. On the third year in bearing wood for next year of three bearing shoots on each side of the bearing stem. In the third year, if the vine is thrifty and well manured—I manure with bone—I let eighteen bunches grow. I consider that no vine in open cultivation ought to have more than twenty pounds; this, with 600 vines to an acre, grows 12,000 pounds of grapes. In 1870 I cut off this patch fifteen tons weight of grapes, but if I had cut seven tons it would have been more money to me, as I was induced to leave too many bearing buds on and thus crippled my vines. I prune in Winter after a heavy frost. At the end of February I tie with twine or wire, disbudding everything except what the vine will be able to bear. I calculate three pounds of grapes to each bearing shoot, and three bunches pay better than five. Unless the wood is overburdened, I do not touch the grapes until I cut them for market. If you are very particular with your vine you 'lath' or 'pinch out.'" Mr. Murtfeldt here showed us the process of lathing or pinching off, which is simply the removal of a shoot by means of a sharp pinch of the forefinger and thumb.

"I like to get the dew off the grapes, as they must be perfectly dry to pack safely. I employ no pickers outside my own family, and this is the rule in this section of the country. The vine will grow in any section. It's the work for women—healthful and congenial. When the grapes are cut (vide illustration), I put 'em into half-bushel baskets and bring 'em to the packing-house. They are then placed on a table and all the poor fruit cut out; then I leave 'em for three or four days to sweat, because when sweated they pack so much better. I have packed forty boxes a day, and so close is the fit that no box would vary from the other a quarter of a pound. I ship all to New York. Ten cents per box is the freight on board; six cents to place it with commission-men, and the commission is ten cents. It costs me eight cents a pound to raise grapes."

This is practically the history of the vine from its being planted to its bearing golden fruit.

For table grapes the soil cannot be too deep or too rich, while twenty inches is the least depth to be relied on, and, if very favorable results are desired, it should be made three feet. Vegetable mold from decayed leaves is considered to be the best invigorator, but as it cannot be always obtained by reason that the leaves require two years before they become sufficiently putrid, rotten wood reduced to a fine mold, the scrapings of the ground in old woods where the trees grow thick together, mold out of hollow trees and sawdust reduced to a fine mold, are substituted. The proper season for planting depends upon local circumstances. The distance apart at which vines should be planted will, of course, depend not only upon the variety but upon the object for which they are set out. In Europe they are placed at all distances, from thirty inches to thirty feet. In the Ohio vineyards, where they are usually fastened to stakes, the plants are placed four and five feet apart; but in the Northern States, where vines are trained upon trellises, they are set in rows six feet apart, the vines standing seven or eight feet apart in the rows. The number of vines required to plant an acre will be seen from the following table:

Plants to the Acre.			Plants to the Acre.		
3 x 3 requires	4,840		8 x 7 requires	788
4 x 3	"	3,630	8 x 8	"	680
4 x 4	"	2,722	9 x 7	"	691
5 x 3	"	2,178	9 x 8	"	605
5 x 5	"	1,742	9 x 9	"	537
6 x 5	"	1,452	10 x 7	"	622
6 x 6	"	1,210	10 x 8	"	544
7 x 6	"	1,023	10 x 9	"	484
7 x 7	"	888	10 x 10	"	435

"Stopping," or pinching, consists in picking off the end of a shoot; its immediate effect is to arrest the further growth of the cane, or at least its further lineal development for the time being. That the leaves are great agents in the elaboration of sap was fully proved by the experiments of Hales, who forced orange flower water into the vessels of a vine, with a view to impart its flavor to the fruit. The experiment was unsuccessful as to the ostensible object, but not as to its concomitant results, for he traced the flavor through the stem and branches to the leaves, but no further; there it was decomposed and doubtless returned to the wood and fruit in the form of sap. When extra fine bunches are desired, one-half the berries should be removed from every bunch, leaving the largest. This operation should be performed when the grapes are about the size of peas. The pruning of vines is reduced to four systems, viz., the long rod renewal system, the long spur syste n, the short or secondary spur system, and the close cut or primary spur system. Viticulturists are now

NEW YORK CITY.—REV. ROBERT COLLYER, NEW PASTOR OF THE CHURCH OF THE MESSIAH.—SEE PAGE 124.

culture was prompting some interesting experimentation.

Since the grapevine, like most living things, reproduces genetically, and each new plant's genes reflect its parents' genes, over the centuries there have been created millions

of varieties or hybrids of *Vitis,* each different in its flavor, its response to soil and climate conditions, and so on. As man learned to use grapes as food and drink, his environment and his preferential choices shaped the evolution of this plant. In western Europe a single strain or family of grapes emerged with a special destiny which its name, *Vitis vinifera* (literally "winemaking grape"), reveals. It was, of course, this European vinifera which so frustratingly refused to grow in the new world.

Caywood and his fellow Hudson region viticulturists deliberately began cross-family genetic blending to develop new hybrid strains, which they reasoned might have the qualities of European "winemakers" and also the disease resistance of the native American grapes. Caywood soon distinguished himself in this work and became a leading authority. He introduced many new hybrid varieties, among them one he named the Dutchess in honor of the county across the river from Marlborough. The exact genetic components of his hybrids are not known, as none of his working records have survived, but according to Mr. Wardell, Dutchess had vinifera parentage. Dutchess had good vineyard characteristics, although it was not quite as disease-free as some other strains that were being introduced at the time by other Hudson hybridizers. It did, however, have outstanding wine quality, which eventually earned it the reputation of being the best wine grape to have its origins in America, a distinction that has not been challenged even today, when it regularly sells for higher prices than any other New York-grown grapes.

Dutchess was not widely accepted in the Hudson region, which may be the reason why Mr. Caywood did not follow up his successful breakthrough and continue emphasizing wine varieties. Perhaps he did try and was simply not successful. In any case, he did not produce any more distinguished wine grapes. His grandson, Mr. Wardell, thought that he had been discouraged by criticism that Dutchess had too tender a skin to ship well and that this and other "practical" considerations had caused the pioneer hybridist to turn his attention away from wine grapes to varieties better suited for other purposes, such as table service and the juice and jelly industries. Wine, after all, was at this point in our pioneer history not considered to be very important. When early settlers had not succeeded in growing European wine grapes during the colonial development period, wine had ceased to be a necessary part of our national diet.

Whatever the reason, Caywood's breakthrough did not lead to a general interest in developing better wine grapes. Nonetheless, the Hudson region grape industry thrived and by 1900 its vineyard acreage had grown to 13,000 acres.

At this point, valley viticulture began a decline for reasons that can be interpreted in different ways. Probably it was due to the fact that, in spite of its excellent climate and soils, crop yields in terms of volume were lower here than in other parts of eastern America. The Hudson's steep terrains, with their troublesome shaly outcroppings, were expensive to cultivate, and the high quality of grapes that could be produced here was not especially important to the juice and jelly processors, who more and more provided the market to which the growers sold their products.

Gradually the practical Hudson region farmers turned to other fruits. Viticulture drifted to the New York Finger Lakes, then into the Middle West, and eventually to California. By the time my family and I arrived in 1957 the Hudson region was largely devoted to bush and tree fruits. Mr. Wardell took a more personal view of the decline and was particularly bitter about the disappearance of grapes along the Hudson. I remember discussing the subject with him one day when we were working in one of the upper vineyards. "Apples," he snorted, looking over the orchard below. "The Dutchess grape could have made this the Rhineland of America, but now look at it; they're growing baby food!"

Whether or not the Dutchess grape was a good enough winemaker to have alone transformed the valley's history may be debatable, but if Mr. Caywood had been inspired to continue his search for still better wine grapes, it is easy to imagine that the Hudson might be among the better-known wine regions of the world today.

Ironically, events were occurring abroad which would have shown Caywood's cross between vinifera and native American species to be extremely far-sighted. At some point during the early 1800s what was often referred to as the American grape blight began to appear in Europe. It is difficult to pin down the date of its commencement because the mysterious malaise was the result of not simply one but numerous diseases, which probably emerged at different times, all almost certainly originating in the new world. It spread like wildfire through France's famous wine lands. By 1885, the year Dutchess was first marketed, the destruction had reached such proportions that it seemed probable that wine as the Europeans made it would disappear from the human diet.

Part of the problem was identified in about 1845 as a fungus infection now called powdery mildew in America, *oidium* in France, and a degree of control was obtained by dusting vineyards with a mixture of sulfur and lime. Then C. V. Riley, an American of English birth working with two Frenchmen, Monsieur Gaston Bazille and Monsieur J. E. Planchon, identified the tiny aphid, native to America, now known as phylloxera, which in one of its many life phases attacked the roots as well as the foliage of European vinifera, as another part of the blight. However, there seemed to be no means for stopping its destructive rampage. Nearly ten more years would pass before a French viticulturist, Albert Seibel, would begin to release cross-pollinated French and American vines as new varieties that were expected to produce the wine quality of vinifera and demonstrate the phylloxera resistance of the American wild varieties.

Once the French began their hybridization experimentation, they persisted with mounting efforts, spurred by a sense of urgency which the non-wine-drinking Hudson grape growers never felt. The French experimenters had another advantage also: they knew what they were looking for in their genetic manipulation—*wine,* sound, good-tasting table wine.

Hybridizing is an agonizingly slow and tedious process, which requires years of work in order to resolve each experimental cross-pollination. First a new variety must be nurtured in the vineyard to fruit-bearing maturity, observed constantly for cultural defects, then its fruit must be vinified, tasted, and evaluated for wine quality. It took many years for satisfactory results to be obtained. Although other means for rehabilitation also emerged, such as grafting vinifera-fruiting varieties onto American rootstocks, slowly

in the late 1800s the phylloxera-devastated French vineyards were replanted, mostly with the new hybrid varieties.

Grafting is a very ancient concept, having been known
at least since Cortez's conquest of Mexico, but it seems
likely that Monsieur Bazille in about 1869 was the earliest
to recommend grafting onto phylloxera-resistant American
vines as a remedy for the devastation of the insect. There is
a commonly heard misunderstanding that the American
vine stock used for rootstock came from California. In fact
it was just about the time of Monsieur Bazille's recommen-
dation that the phylloxera epidemic moved west across the
Rockies and attacked the vinifera varieties planted there
with the same ferocity it had shown in Europe. The successful rootstock material instead came entirely from sources
east of the Rockies, and the most effective varieties were
those of the riparia, aestivalis and rotundifolia species. Labrusca vines, often mistakenly given the credit for service as
a resistant rootstock, are in fact not immune to phylloxera.

Grafting the old vinifera vines onto American rootstock
came to be preferred for replanting in the most famous vineyard areas, such as Bordeaux and Burgundy, where the
growers had a traditional commitment to the classic varieties. However, the hybrids became very popular everywhere
else. They produced good crops of grapes, which frequently
made better wine than the old varieties, with less work, and
they were less expensive to plant and less susceptible to
vineyard diseases than the grafted vinifera. By 1958 over
two-thirds, nearly a million acres, of the French nation's
total vineyard was planted in new hybrid varieties.

The success of the hybrids led to a curious confrontation, however. In the 1900s politically powerful grape growers in southern France and French Algeria, whose vinifera
vines produced vast amounts of cheap bulk wines (generally
mediocre in quality) felt threatened by the growing acreage
of the hybrids, and they succeeded in obtaining government
restrictions to curtail their planting. Consequently, since
about 1960 there has been a decline in hybrid acreage in

favor of grafted vinifera, even though the vinifera in many cases is of inferior quality. Resistance to the political pressure is still strong, however, and the hybrids today account for a portion of French wine production exceeding the entire production of California.

At Benmarl we were considering both the hybrids and the vinifera. By mid-January we were steeped in the lore of the Hudson region viticultural saga and my light-hearted hobby had taken on a certain burden of responsibility. I had come to feel that this old piece of land, which had outlived all of its early contemporaries and remained now as the oldest and last of America's pioneer vineyards, had its unfulfilled destiny ahead of it and we had become its stewards, with an obligation to carry on the research begun by its founder.

It didn't matter that most of our fellow Hudson farmers had chosen to grow apples. I felt that we had found an ideal place to grow wine grapes. After all, the climate was the same and the soil was the same as it had been two hundred years earlier when cultivated grapevines had found their first safe haven in the new world. In that span of time, a lot had happened. Now there were sprayers to control fungus diseases. The mysterious vine blight was now known to be an insect, which could be thwarted by grafting any desired fruiting vine onto a tougher resistant rootstock. Along with the classic vinifera varieties there were now dozens of exciting new crossbred varieties, proven to be good winemakers elsewhere, all just waiting to be tried here.

Dene, a bit wryly, observed that all this experimentation sounded expensive for a young family with two children, a budding career, and only a modest income. As usual, her prediction would prove to be right, but nothing was going to deter me at this point.

chapter IV

Our First Year

I learned from Mr. Wardell that the calendar of spring labors for a Hudson region grape grower is likely to begin in late winter, when a break in the mid-February weather permits him to begin pruning his vines. Discussion with the Extension Service agent revealed that some local growers of hardy varieties such as Concord even started this work the previous autumn after the leaves fell. Of course we had been too busy with our land-reclamation program then. Milton, upon whom the major burden of this work would fall, assured me that there would be enough time. However, February 15 came and went with no opportunity for him to begin. I telephoned him every night from our Hartsdale residence, hoping that somehow the cold, wet winter we were having in Westchester might somehow be different in Ulster. Where was that Roman sun we should be basking under? My uneasiness was no doubt obvious to my sons, then eight and ten years old. Kim, the older, ran into my home studio one evening and thrust the *Pogo* comic strip into my hands, pointing to the balloon above the wise little possum saying, "We isn't ever gone see spring ifn we don't stop buying our winters from Canada." We laughed about it and made up our minds to get started on the pruning this weekend "weather or no."

Actually, the winter had been well spent in terms of practical accomplishment as well as in the shaping of our idealistic goals. Since frozen ground had forced a halt to vineyard repair work, I had occupied my weekends and whatever other time I could spare with the heavier work of renovating the farmhouse interior, stripping the old paper off the walls and sanding the floors, which turned out to be of good quality and quite pretty when cleaned. I was determined to make the place look as nice as possible by spring so that Dene could begin painting and redecorating when I moved to field work.

Until autumn I had managed to keep her misgivings about our purchase just barely below the level of despair by optimistic projections about how much fun it would be to turn our little "sow's ear into a silk purse." From an aerial photo of the farm I painted a picture showing its grungy structures beautifully rebuilt and repainted, pristine white and brilliant against a green, well-mowed lawn. The fourteen old cherry trees scattered among the buildings were handsome in full leaf, the vineyards neat. The five-acre portion of the property upon which the residences, barn, and other outbuildings were set I surrounded with a trim white-washed rail fence, and the farm entrance was flanked by two gateposts. Very pretty. I took every opportunity to point out how splendid it would be for the boys to have a truly rural environment in which to develop their skills of self-reliance, and how fortunate that those sweet cherry trees were there. They would obviously solve our financial problems. Based upon the Extension agent's estimated yield for an average tree and the prices paid during the previous year, we would easily earn enough to cover the mortgage, meet the farm's renovation expenses, and probably start a savings fund for the boys' college education.

When the leaves fell, however, the tired old place stood

stark and grim, stripped of the remotest semblance of the
charm my painting suggested. Even my dogged optimism
sagged. How had I failed to notice before that, in addition
to the desperate need for paint on the sides of the house, the
old-fashioned metal roof was also bare and actually rusted
through in a number of places. That explained the disinte-
grated plaster in the back stairway hall. A dreaded investiga-
tion showed that not only had the plaster been soaked and
ruined but the very sills supporting the wall were rotted!

The summer leaves had also helped conceal the fact that
the window shutters were hopelessly gapped from missing
louvers and all hung askew. But this sort of minor cosmetic
flaw was forgotten as other problems arose.

For a while we had considered actually using the old
cast-iron stove in the kitchen. Mrs. Edith Caywood Meckes
had a similar one in her delightful old-fashioned farm
kitchen. It looked charming and quaint. Examination
showed, however, that ours was badly cracked and, although it was repairable, it would be a burden to maintain,
so we decided to replace it with an ordinary modern gas
range. I tried to sell it, but young Bruno deLuca, a local
antique dealer, persuaded me that it was not worth anything
to anyone but him. It would be better for me to trade it to
him for the trouble of removing it. Much of that trouble
turned out to be mine. We backed his flat-bed truck carefully against the high porch and jacked it up to the exact
level of the porch floor so that the stove could be dollied
directly onto the truck. The stove was too wide to pass
through the kitchen door so it had to be tilted onto the dolly
by rigging a block and tackle to the ceiling joist. The floor
sagged noticeably when the full weight of the stove was
lowered onto the dolly. We quickly rolled it outside. A
porch plank cracked—but held. Suddenly the jack-sup-
ported truck sagged against the porch. The brick foundation
post gave way, the entire porch floor tipped, the stove
pitched down the incline, and its ornate cast-iron body shattered like a clay pot.

So it went, but at last the heaviest renovating was done. The old coal furnace in the cellar was dismantled and replaced by an efficient oil-burning model. A minor contretemps developed from this. Having been out of service during the years Mr. Wardell had relied on the kitchen stove for "central heating," the hot-water radiators promptly sprang leaks in numerous places, but that had been anticipated and the breaks were quickly sealed. The floors were shellacked and waxed. The walls were sized for repapering, the ceilings replastered, and the kitchen floor brightened with sturdy linoleum.

Pogo's complaint apparently impressed whoever bought our winter weather. One late February evening the snow stopped, and on Saturday morning early, Dene, Kim, Eric, and I piled into the four-wheel-drive Jeep in Hartsdale and saw the sun rise forty minutes later at the farm. The promise of winter's end, if not exactly the arrival of spring, was definitely in the air. There was a lot of recent snow on the ground, however, and we were only able to drive a short distance into our property along a hand-shoveled path just wide enough for a car. Milton didn't have a car himself, but he kept the pathway open for us and so that his friends could drive in and out and do his meager marketing for him. He also kept the pathway open across the nearly three hundred yards separating his house and mine so that he could check on things there while we were away, and he shoveled another to the barn. I wondered why he troubled to keep this last path cleared and idly assumed it was a compulsion left over from the days when a horse had been kept there and required daily attention. It was only years later, after he died, that I found a more likely reason: while tearing out a partition in the barn's cellar, I exposed a stash of home-distilled brandy. It was very good.

Milton was extremely self-reliant. He spent almost nothing on food, obtaining virtually everything he needed from a small garden behind his house and regular hunting with his hounds. Each year he preserved a large store of beans, potatoes, and fruits. He slaughtered a hog periodically and kept its meat salted, hanging in his cellar with the other preserves. Each autumn he always made some applejack and a little wine from the Delaware grapes. The wine he drank almost immediately because by Christmas it began to turn vinegary. He was fussier about his apple brandy and chose only certain varieties for the basic distilling material. He stored the young brandy and drank only that which had been stored for a few years. He never really learned to like the wines I made, which, even when I had nothing but the Delaware grape to work with, were made dry. His was, at the first of the season, very very sweet and remained fizzy and cloudy until gradually it reached an alcohol content too high to permit further fermentation. Then it cleared and slowly began to turn sour. He liked it in all stages, and when it finally became too vinegary to drink, he used it for cooking and for medicinal purposes. For example, he made a balm for his chronic "arthuritis" by dissolving used steel needles (the finest steel was necessary, he said) in a large mason jar of his vinegar. This took a few weeks but he could start using it when about half the metal disappeared. He applied it with a rag three or four times a day during attacks, rubbing it into his swollen knee joints vigorously. He claimed it gave unfailing relief.

Milton saw us arrive and met us at our car. On occasions like this I plowed out the snow-covered roads around the property with the farm tractor and the blade terracer. He had everything ready, the tractor fitted with chains and the blade attached. We had never bought a snow-plow attachment for the jeep because we didn't need it in Hartsdale and we were usually at the farm only on weekends during the snowy months. Plowing took only an hour, then the boys and I set out up the steep hill to begin pruning the high vineyards, leaving Milton to work in the ones near the house.

All the vines on the farm were trained fairly low onto two wires, one about thirty inches from the ground and the

upper about sixteen to eighteen inches higher. This seemed
to be the management also employed by most other growers
in the area. In vigorous vineyards a "four-cane Kniffin"
system was widely used: two "heads," or areas where shoots
were encouraged to emerge, were established at the wire
levels, and every season two one-year canes were selected
from each head to be extended and tied to the wires, one to

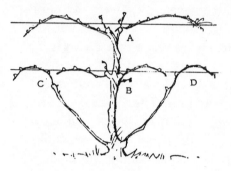

1. *Pruned vine at beginning of season.*   2. *Same vine repruned for next season.*

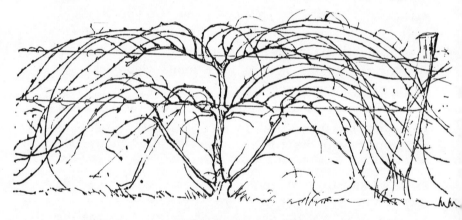

3. *Same vine at end of season.*

the right, the other to the left. The length of the canes and
the number of fruiting buds left on them to produce the
coming season's fruit were decided by the pruner. His decision was critical because it determined the upper limits of
the year's crop. Local farmers made this decision by "eye-

balling it," they said, judging by experience and the way grandpa had done it. A total of thirty-five buds on a vine would produce a yield around eight to ten pounds, or two and a half to three tons per acre in good years.

The old Delawares I was confronting had received so little care in recent years that they had low vigor and very little cane growth. Milton and I had decided to try rebuilding them next season so we left only two canes, both on the top wire, with just six buds each. The pruned vines were not retied to the wires. That would come later. With so little previous growth to remove, work went fast. It became tedious to Kim and Eric, though, and they went down the hill to search out an old bobsled they had seen in the barn's attic. The deep snow was dazzling, reflecting the brilliant sunlight back from the ground as intensely as it shone from the sky. I would have a Florida tan soon, from the neck up. I had brought a sandwich and stayed at my work until the sun got low and my feet, wet from perspiration inside heavy socks and boots, began to feel very cold. As I started home and looked back over the day's work I could see that Milton had been right. We would easily finish before planting time. Dene had prepared a chicken tetrazzini on the new stove, so we drew off a small pitcher of the wine made from the Delaware grapes given to us by Mr. Wardell when we bought the farm. The combination was astonishingly good, and variations on this dish became our favorites during the years we grew and drank Delaware wine.

In the middle 1950s there were still many farm animals in use in the Hudson region. Our farm had done most of the cultivation with a horse. Many of our neighbors had cows. Many also had chickens. The availability of animal manure was such that most grape growers used this natural fertilizer, which was free for the asking, rather than buy the more expensive manufactured ones. I didn't know many local people and was on the point of ordering the granular nitrogen I had used on my Hartsdale garden when Milton insisted that instead one of his friends would bring over four large wagonloads of chicken droppings—enough for all the upper vineyards. "No charge cep'n for haulin'." I had cleaned out our small chicken house when I was a boy in Oklahoma and the memory of it, though dimmed by time, made me hesitate before agreeing, but Milton's pride in saving us "a pile of money" was so obvious that I didn't object.

When I arrived on Friday afternoon he could hardly wait for me to see the delivered fertilizer. Before it came in sight the pungent smell of ammonia reminded me of why I had hesitated. "How will you spread it?" I asked when we stood looking up at the enormous hill of manure. He clearly heard the "you" in my question and he stroked his chin a number of times before answering, "Why, uh—I, uh—" He knew I could see there really wasn't any way it could be done with our limited equipment except to shovel it by hand onto our trailer and then throw it off again under the vine trellises, shovelful by shovelful, as the tractor pulled it along each row. The next morning he had the trailer hitched to the tractor and was waiting for me at the barn, shovel in hand. He was wearing an old pair of fisherman's hip boots over coveralls, and a large bandana was knotted around his neck, ready to be pulled up over his nose. "You jus' drive," he said. All I had been able to improvise for protective covering was snow boots, old clothes, and a worn-out spray mask without its filter, which I had found in my cellar and stuffed with a rag. We set out for the "pile of savings" on the hill. I made him let me take my turn shoveling, though it meant putting the tractor in place myself at the end of each row, helping him to mount it, favoring his "game leg." He could then manage to "guide" the tractor on the straight run. Then we would repeat the process after I had turned the tractor around for him at the end of the row. We kept grimly at it for the entire weekend, our backs aching, eyes smarting. Even Milton's work-hardened hands were blistered. Mine were bleeding—and the smell . . . there was no way to wash thoroughly enough to get the memory of it out of my nostrils for weeks after. Milton had a sense of humor. When we got so tired we just numbly pushed ourselves on, he began to make what I call old minstrel-show jokes—nothing original: "I tole my mother I was gwine be a pilot. Yah, she say —I know, you gwine pile it here, then you gwine pile it there." But they made it possible to finish the job.

Tying vines is a nice job. It doesn't require a complicated knot, just enough to hold the vine on the wire, and is generally the last handwork of the spring season. The weather is usually mild by then. The birds are back. The apple-tree wood is red in the valley below. The shad trees' white blossoms scatter smoky puffs over the hills rimming the valley floor. Old residents told me that in earlier days willow wands were gathered and used for tying vines. Valley farmers now used balls of rough grass twine which is stocked by the local hardware store.

I had always carried the unraveling twine ball in a pocketed carpenter's apron when tying my Hartsdale vines, but Milton simply dropped his down the front of his shirt and threaded the string out between buttons at his waist, which was conveniently about the height of the wire to which we tied the vines. He was incredibly fast at throwing the cord around a trunk or cane and tying a knot using only one hand, the other carrying his razor-sharp pocket knife with which he snipped off the umbilical twine to move to the next vine. When we first began to work together we would start on adjacent rows, one above the other, and he would pass in front of me three or four times, doing one row after another while I was able to tie only one. Gradually I picked up speed, but he had reserves of experience and a will to compete, and he never let me truly catch up to him. I really preferred to tie alone, moving at my own pace and enjoying the magnificent sight of the burgeoning valley spread panoramically below.

Actually, before a vineyard could be tied, the posts which heaved out during the spring thaw had to be driven back in and then the wires to support the vines drawn taut. The posts were driven with a twelve-pound sledgehammer

with a large striking face or a large wooden maul. I made myself a little step stool to carry with me in order to gain enough height to swing the hammer squarely onto the top of the posts. A glancing blow could split a post. Milton was tall enough to do it without a stool and consequently was twice as fast. Even with the slowing effect of my unpracticed efforts, we were able to make good progress. Nonetheless, the vines we had ordered from Philip Wagner's Boordy Vineyards' nursery came before we finished. We put them in the coolest recesses of the barn cellar and redoubled our efforts, with Dene and the boys tying, while Milton and I pounded posts and tightened wire from daybreak till dark.

Before it was finished, Milton and I put our weekends to planting, leaving the other work altogether to the others. Although the weather had been cooperative for most of our spring weekends, now it turned against us—from the standpoint of comfort anyway. It rained. We had prepared our land for planting by plowing a deep furrow for each row, then turning the soil back into the furrow from both sides, creating a hill of loose, easy-to-dig soil to plant in. There were so many stony spots and shaly outcroppings that the field could not be laid out very precisely. We simply used a stick cut to a seven-foot length as an approximate spacer between plants, and dug. If we hit rock we moved a few feet

or inches until we could make an adequate hole. The rain, even though only a drizzle, turned our plowed fields to a quagmire. We slogged through it, one man making a hole for each plant with a spade, the other following on his knees in the muck to plant each vine. In following years we improved our techniques for planting or, at any rate, we developed faster ways to do the work. This first season, under the pressure of a time schedule growing steadily tighter as the weather grew warmer and our unplanted vines began to push out unhealthy-looking spindly white shoots in their dark barn storage, we doggedly did the best we could. And, as all our other problems had yielded to our persistence, this one did as well and we at last finished. As the summer came our little vines grew as happily as if they had been planted by experts. Of course the weeds did too.

Milton knew what to do about that. "Buy a hoss!" he said. With a turning plow and some equine power he would handle the weeds as he always had in the past. This time, though, I insisted that we look for a more modern solution. We had a good tractor after all. Okay, *I* could be the "hoss." Riding the tractor, I would pull the plow as he guided it. We tried it and after a while we got pretty good at it. However, the system was not very labor efficient. It took two men to function and I was only available on weekends. The weeds, uncooperatively, grew all week long. Milton got out the old

grape hoe he had used for years. When the "hoss" was in the city painting pictures Milton grubbed away at the weeds alone. My city work kept me busy during the week and the only advisors I had time to consult with on weekends were the old-time grape growers in the village who were friends of Mr. Wardell. He brought them over to meet me and look at my problem. "Get a horse," they all agreed.

I was reluctant to give in to this advice. Even though we had an excellent barn for the purpose, the smelly horse stall was adjacent to the cool barn cellar, which I planned to make my winery. The two uses just weren't compatible. I knew there must be better ways. I had seen them in France. My dilemma was resolved by the need to drive, one Saturday morning, to a neighboring town for a tractor part. I passed a vineyard and saw a man operating a tool that functioned in principle very much like our horse-pulled plow except that it was mounted on the side of the tractor. With it he was able to throw a small berm of soil toward his vine, covering weed growth, then later cut the berm out, taking the new growth with it. His was hand-operated but there were newer versions powered by the tractor's hydraulic system. I ordered one through State Sarles Sons, a local garage, which also serviced tractors. I told Esmond Sarles how fortunate I had been to find this solution to my weed problem.

"Could've told you if you'd asked," he said. Encouraged by finding a new source of advice, I posed another problem to him. Because of our earlier reliance on chicken manure, I had failed to order manufactured fertilizer, which I found I needed for the cherry trees. Now the local supplier was out of stock. "What would you suggest?" He pretended to think awhile. "Most folks around here grow their own," he said with a grin. "Ever think of getting a horse?"

The hydraulic "grape hoe" was a godsend, although our rocky ground kept it in the shop frequently for repairs during the first few years, until gradually all the heavy stones had been uncovered and removed from the zone under the trellis in which it operated.

In early June the grapevine flowers in the Hudson Valley as a kind of elegant climax to the intense early spring labors. This is not a spectacular event. In fact it is rather anticlimactic. All the tree fruits have completed their showy blossoming weeks before. It occurs some five to six weeks

after leaves have appeared on the vines and shoots are eighteen inches to two feet long. The grape flower is a tiny yellow blossom, which could easily be missed by the eye of an inexperienced passerby—but the fragrance! Subtle yet insistently pervasive, innocently fresh yet containing more seductive notes of earthy, musklike character. The thought comes to mind that this little flower would surely become the source for a fabulous perfume if it weren't for the fact that it has a greater destiny to fulfill. No, this perfume will never be discreetly dabbed behind your lady's ear but will have to be carried by the memory from year to year.

By the end of spring the pace of the vineyard activities slowed a bit. Oh, there was plenty to do and new problems of almost crisis intensity continued to arise. The old wooden tank sprayer which I had hoped to put into service proved to be unrepairable. I built a duster to use powdered fungicides, but unless the vines were wet with early-morning dew the powder didn't stick well to the leaves. Finally we had to rig a sprayer from a small Meyers pump, installed directly on the power-takeoff drive shaft, and a weird assembly of plumbing pipe fitted with catalogue-ordered spray nozzles. It worked adequately. The apple farmers had powerful air-blast sprayers available to them but I wasn't able to find one small enough for our vineyards. Nonetheless, there was a feeling of lessened urgency.

Occasionally there was a moment to walk alone through the green vines, enjoying the crunch of the slaty soil under my boots, softened by the thick foot-high daisies that sprang up voluntarily between the vine rows of the upper vineyards. This was a little more like the *vigneron*'s life I had imagined.

My respite was short. The cherries would ripen in a few days' time. We had managed to keep them in pretty good condition. Brown rot, a fungus that was our major problem, had been controlled by sulfur blasted onto the trees by the same duster device we temporarily had used in the vineyards and then later by a high-pressure, hand-held spray gun when our rigged sprayer had been built.

Our variety of trees ripened their fruit about two or three weeks before school was out, which I had considered to be unfortunate because it would deny us a cheaper labor force. Milton was not concerned, saying that kids wouldn't be able to handle the forty-foot ladders anyway. He had many friends who knew exactly what to do and they needed the work. There certainly was no denying the last part. The nearby town of Newburgh, which had once been a prosperous and handsome old city, serving the needs of one of the nation's leading fruit-producing industries and a booming riverboat commerce as well, was rapidly becoming a depressed ghetto of unemployed workers whose numbers had grown enormously after World War II.

Milton gave his friends the word that we would have to begin Saturday morning. Five carloads arrived at 7 A.M., thirty-six people altogether, counting their babies and children of school age—about twice as many as we had expected. We had ladders for only about fifteen of them, but Milton was loath to turn anyone away. "Our cherries is very ripe," and we'd better "git 'em off" as fast as possible. So the more agile took over the ladders while others picked what they could reach from the ground. The older people worked in the barn packing cherries for market. It was a colorful sight, and a general mood of cheerful good humor prevailed. By the end of the day we had a good load for the Quimby brothers' truck to take to the Manhattan market. I wanted to continue picking right through the weekend because we had discovered that the fruit on some trees was so ripe that it was deteriorating. By Monday we could have these trees completely harvested and would be able to get by with a normal smaller, week-day work force. I suggested that we pay for the whole weekend on Sunday night so as to have fewer checks to write, but the idea met with such complaint that I relented and paid everyone fully Saturday evening, $576.40 all told. Everyone swore on a stack of Bibles they would be back at seven the next morning. When nine o'-clock came, then ten came and went without a single soul showing up, not even Milton, I knew my overripe cherries were destined to be eaten by the birds.

The Quimbys called to report that the prices had been down last night and that our fruit was a little soft. The whole load had brought $459, less hauling and broker's commissions, which left us with a net of $329, meaning a loss of $247.40.

Shortly after noon, a beat-up white 1948 Cadillac drove up with two of my erstwhile pickers. They swayed tipsily toward Milton's house and were knocking on his door when I walked over to meet them. The old man came out walking feebly, clearly hung over. "My arthuritis actin' up again," he said to me. "Where are the rest?" he asked of the two in a low voice. The answer came back, "Cleatus is in jail. Everybody else is sick." I could see it would be hopeless to try to do any work today.

Monday morning I called my office to arrange a time extension on a job expected to be delivered and helped a contrite Milton set up the ladders in the trees to be picked that day. By eight o'clock no pickers had arrived. "I know where to find some folks willing to work," Milton said. We drove to Newburgh, then from one house to another, collecting a motley crew. By ten-thirty we had them in the trees. All was quiet except for the soft "thunk" of cherries being dropped in the tin pails hooked to the ladders' rungs. By four o'clock they all climbed down.

"Kind of short day today," observed the trucker when he came to pick up the shipment to take to market. I nodded. "Maybe the prices will be high."

He was wrong. When the last cherry was in and the last check received from the broker, the total earnings for the entire hectic period, net of all expenses, not counting a broken ladder, was $85—loss. Dinner was quiet that evening. "Well, the boys are not near college age yet," I said, but Dene's smile was a little wan.

At this early stage in our association with our new property we referred to it as "the farm." Then one night, with the help of a friend, I came up with its present name.

Jack Jackson was a Scotsman with a brogue so thick "you'd have to cut it with a bloody sword," as he said of himself. He loved to drink, preferably beer or good Scotch whisky, but out of regard for me, after we bought the vineyard, he said from now on he would take "a wee glass of wine now and again to see if I can acquire a tolerance for the stuff." He thought it was "daft to throw good money after bad" on a project such as my farm but he insisted on coming up to help me out with the work. Today when I tell the story of how we got the name "Benmarl," I say, "It's a combination of two Gaelic words we found one night at the bottom of a bottle." When Jack and I came in from a hot afternoon's work one weekend, when our wives had not come along to keep us civilized, we decided we were too tired to cook and too dirty to go out so we sat down and opened some wine, and, with a large piece of cheese and some bread, proceeded to put away the bottle in a few gulps, opened another and then another. The farther we got into slaking our thirst the more Gaelic Jack's speech became. There were five corks lying on the table when, "I've got it!" he exclaimed, just about two inches from the bottom of the bottle, "the name for this bloody stony mountain you squeezed this loovely stuff from." "Tell me," I said. "Benmarrl," he replied, pronouncing it slowly in a hoarse whisper, rolling his r-r-r's dramatically—" 'Ben' for hill and 'marl' for the bloody slaty rock it's made of." We poured the last drops from the bottle for a toast to "slate hill." *"Les amours de la bouteille** salute the wines of the future Benmarl!" And so we've called it since that day. Even though virtually no one has ever understood it on first pronunciation, it was Jack's "bloody" name for it and I liked it. Today we think it's one of our greatest assets. People say, "It was so hard to learn to pronounce it I could never forget it."

To say that the rest of the summer passed peacefully would be an exaggeration. More accurately, it passed without serious mishap. Every day spent at the farm was an

---

**Les amours de la bouteille*—the last loving drops from the bottle.

intense learning experience. Problems arose and solutions were found, or invented. Mr. Wardell and his eagerly helpful old retired farmer cronies were never reluctant to give advice, but their ideas were most often based on experience gained from the deep past and usually required some tool or piece of equipment no longer available. Milton, of course, tended to think in outdated terms as well, but he was always there to hold the other end of the plank, so to speak, as we muddled our way through, and between us we re-invented almost everything but the wheel.

By harvest time I had built a little winery in the barn with shelves for the five-gallon glass carboys. There were now two fifty-gallon refurbished whiskey barrels on sturdy racks against the wall. Another slightly larger sixty-five gallon brandy barrel, given to me by Julius Wile of the famous importing firm, was mounted end up with the top removed to serve as a fermenting vat. It was placed on a castered dolly so that it could be moved about from place to place, first to the roofed-over shed where the tractor could pull up its little trailer load of baskets filled with grapes. A used hand-powered grape crusher bought from an old Italian man I had met at the grape market had been adapted to clamp firmly onto the fermenter. One person slowly dumped the grape baskets into the crusher's hopper while another turned its roller handle, crushing the grapes, which fell directly into the up-ended barrel. When filled, the small vat could be covered and rolled inside into the cool barn for a three- to ten-day fermentation, then pushed back outside to a little hand press, which would yield a little under ten gallons of wine for each load.

Another prize piece of equipment was a rebuilt bench corker made by the Demoisy company in Beaune. Really French! It was bound to add quality to my wines. I had an electric pump, which was mostly a decoration since the volume of my production was so small that my two or three stainless milk pails were more than adequate for moving the liquids from one place to another. It was gorgeous! And the

barn cellar was a splendid place for it. The cellar had originally been built in the 1800s as a cooler to keep fruit fresh
until it could conveniently be shipped to market on the
paddle-wheel steamboats plying the Hudson in those days.
Its walls and ceiling were insulated with ten to twelve inches
of shredded cork covered by planking. There were two large
similarly insulated doors. The refrigerant in early days was
ice. The Hudson River froze solid during winter. Horses and
wagons were driven out onto it and great blocks of ice were
carved out, to be hauled back to the barn coolers of the
region. In a well-built example such as ours, Mr. Wardell
said, there would be adequate refrigeration to get through a
whole year.

Grapes were picked with the aid of small scissorlike
clippers or with ring knives similar to those used for string
cutting today. A person with strong fingernails and tough
hands could learn to grasp the grape cluster's stem at just the
right point and snap it off cleanly without any tools at all.
Milton did this very well. My nails are paper thin and brit-
tle, so they stayed broken and split as I forced myself to pick
as he did.

Milton was ready to pick long before I would let the
harvest begin. His experience had been in harvesting for the
table-grape market. The Caywood-Wardell Delawares had
made a name for themselves in the New York City and
Albany markets and were even known as far away as Bos-
ton. They were picked at the peak of their cosmetic perfec-

tion rather than wine perfection and sorted carefully on long tables, the prettiest going into twelve-pound handled baskets, just like those we had used for packing cherries, and shipped to those markets.

I taught him to gather a random sample of ripening grapes, squeeze them into a tubular jar, then determine their sugar content with a balling saccharometer, a process I had learned when I first began making wines in Hartsdale. This device was virtually the only piece of equipment among my panoply of prizes that was new and not secondhand. Bought at Milan Laboratories on Spring Street in New York City, it had dramatically changed the success rate of my winemaking activities. It looks much like a large thermometer with a long, thin stem, but instead of a mercury sump at one end it has a bulb filled with lead shot. Lowered carefully into the jar, the shot-weighted end would sink to a level determined by the sugar content of the grape juice and this could be read directly as a percentage from numbers appearing on the saccharometer's stem. Since grape sugar is converted by fermentation into a fairly predictable amount of alcohol, the device permitted me to decide on the optimum time to start harvesting our crop. As the grapes approached wine maturity Milton would do this every day and I would call him to learn the results of his tests each evening from the city or from our Hartsdale home.

One of the more pleasant aspects of our new hobby was that it was an instant conversation starter, even though in 1957 wine was not the enormously popular refreshment it is today. In fact, it was very rarely served with food except in Italian homes or those of sophisticated and well-traveled people. It was hard to find good wines in neighboring package stores, and most who carried them had only a very limited stock to choose from. We found, however, that almost everyone had a great amount of curiosity about wine, and we were flattered to oblige with accounts of our limited but very personal experience. Conversations usually led to an invitation to visit us, rejoined by "Let me know when you're picking grapes. I'll come and help."

Milton, of course, had his friends all poised for the signal to harvest, but our experience during the cherry season made me less than enthusiastic about this prospective labor force. When I notified our friends that the time had come, their response was enthusiastic, and they swarmed upon the farm armed with their own shears and household scissors. There was such a small crop that first year that the whole harvest, all Delaware grapes, was accomplished in a few hours. We crushed and pressed enough to make a barrel for ourselves and our crew of volunteers. The rest were saved to sell to home winemakers who had arranged to come by the following day. Tired, but very pleased with ourselves, we spread a marvelous buffet picnic under the cherry trees on the long grape-sorting tables. Bottles of the previous year's vintage were spread out liberally between the platters of food. A small barrel of fresh apple cider was fitted with a spigot so the youngsters could serve themselves. Fatigue disappeared with the first few bottles, and an obvious mood of satisfaction warmed into gaiety—and I imagined a special sense of fellowship. Darkness came, and we lit the area with kerosene torches, but the chill of a September evening finally began to thin the ranks of our amateur bacchic revelers. Dene and I waved the last of them off and walked, tired again, silently back to the farmhouse.

For me it had been an inspiring day. I felt an odd sense of . . . almost exultation, very much the same feeling that

sometimes came with the completion of a well-constructed, well-painted picture. It wasn't smugness, nor even particularly self-congratulation—just a comforting sense of being one step closer to one's goal. But . . . why should I feel this way now? This day's pleasant achievement was only for fun. This old grape farm was just a hobby . . . or was it becoming something else? Was there also a certain feeling of penance? The guilty knowledge that, as the oldest son, much had been planned for me by my family, which I had rejected by becoming an artist, had always burdened my conscience.

My grandfather, Richard Marshall Thorp, had acquired a substantial land holding in his lifetime. He had, as a young man, stood on the border of Oklahoma Territory the day it was opened for homesteading and at the gunshot signal driven his wagon hellbent to stake out a claim. He had been driven off his first two claims at gunpoint by marauders and had ridden on until he succeeded. He had farmed the land and bought more land with his earnings. R. M., as he was generally known by his friends, was a patriarch of the town where I grew up. A man of very few words, he was a pillar of the church, a willing supporter and source of funds for any benefit to the community. I was his first grandchild. From the day I could sit erect in an automobile seat he had taken me with him on his daily tours of the family's farms. Cotton and wheat were, for the most part, their cash crops, and to grow them profitably required large parcels of land. A four- to five-section farm was not considered unusually large. A section was one square mile.

Granddad bought a new Ford coupé every year, always black and as long as they were made, always with a "jump seat," which I never saw anyone use. We would set out in the morning by six o'clock and drive across the prairie past miles of plow-combed fields. Presently he would slow down, pull over to the edge of the unpaved road, and we would sit looking out across the pan-flat plain, waiting, usually without conversation, listening to the soft moan of the constant prairie winds. Often a buzzard or an eagle soared in the cloudless sky. It is only in retrospect that I realize we didn't talk much to each other because there was always a sense of total communication. Sometimes we got out of the car and he would walk a few hundred feet up a row, examining whatever crop was being grown, pick up a handful of dirt, and crumble it through his fingers, smell it, taste it, then wipe his tongue with a handkerchief. After a while he would pull out his gold pocket watch, then shade his eyes with his hand and peer out over the field, whistling softly to himself. I don't remember the tune ever changing. It was always "That Strawberry Roan."

Without ever having to think why, I always knew who we were waiting for. Also I knew why we had stopped at this particular place. The freshly turned furrow there on the right meant that somewhere along that row Brad McKinnon was plowing toward its western end, perhaps three miles away, and that eventually a little cloud of dust on the horizon would indicate that he was working his way back toward us. The two men would talk for a while and then we would drive to our next rendezvous, also marked only by some difference in the appearance of the dirt in the vast fields that told us where the target of our visit would presently appear.

I was named Marshall after my grandfather, but since he was always referred to as R. M., when I heard the name on these trips I knew it referred to me. Often at the end of one of Granddad's conversations the farmer would say, "Marshall, come on ovah heah. Ah've got somethin' you'll like," and I would immediately be alert and follow over to a watermelon patch. The farmer would take out a large pocket knife, plunge it deep into a striped melon and cut out a large plug. If the end of the plug was deep red, he would snap it off the vine and thrust the huge three-foot-long giant into my arms. "Y'all take this along home with you."

Once I remember we found our man near his house. It was close to dinnertime, which meant the noon meal, and we were invited in. Carl Hemmer was a German who had come

from the old country and had homesteaded, as my grandfather had, in the opening run of the Oklahoma Territory. He grew a few grapes and made his own wine. Granddad was a teetotaler because Grandmother was a teetotaler, but he had grown up on a grape farm in Missouri and his family had made wine. He picked up the plain glass tumbler that Carl's wife set before him, touched it to Carl's extended glass, and took a token sip. Carl understood and asked nothing more, but put a second tumbler, this one filled with water, by my grandfather's plate and one filled with fresh milk near mine. When Carl picked up his glass again and drank I looked up at my grandfather and lifted his forbidden glass, smelled it and sipped the sweet fragrance of wine for the first time in my life. I started to sip again but Granddad put his hand gently on my shoulder and I put the glass down. That was my first taste of wine. Now I was growing grapes and making my own.

Dene and I walked together to extinguish the torches. She, I knew, felt different about the day that had given me such warm satisfaction. The money, the time spent on this hobby could have been better used, she thought, to further my real career. Lately I had turned down well-paying but minor commissions to spend weekends with my grapes.

But for me painting had become a highly pressured business. Often a picture would be recomposed and re-painted a dozen times before I would submit it. Often I would paint for days on end with little sleep to meet a publishing deadline. I must have been a terrible father during such times, and an even worse husband. After delivering a painting I desperately needed to get to the farm to unwind, to swing a heavy maul or climb on a tractor and drive under the hot sun until sweat poured and the steady drone of the engine gradually relaxed tense muscles and dilated the perceptions of the brain so sharply focused on the abstract orchestrations of color, composition, and characterization that it simply couldn't function in other ways. My contemporaries developed ulcers or worse. My farm, although it often kept me from my matrimonial and paternal responsibilities, at least kept me sane and reasonably healthy.

Perhaps also, I thought tonight, it kept me in touch with my grandfather and the deep unspoken love for land and for growing things he had shared with me as a child. My life might have followed in his footsteps, as he had hoped, but the great drought and the winds of the 1930s, which blew away their farms and forced so many thousands of Oklahomans to California, also lured me away to explore other ways of life. Grandfather stayed and prospered again, but I had broken the faith and couldn't go home again.

chapter V

Growth and Change

The following year, in spite of Dene's reservations, we
moved to the farm. It was becoming too expensive to maintain two residences as well as my studio in Manhattan. In
addition, because of the changes in the magazine industry
due to television and photography which I mentioned earlier, art commissions were scarcer and scarcer. At the same
time I was also trying to find sources for funds to contribute
to the rising costs of operating the farm. We were now
carrying on a sizable empirical research program, which I felt
could have considerable impact on Hudson Valley agriculture. We were making progress toward producing good
wine, although the scale of our operations was very small.
Now entering their third year, the vineyards we had planted

at Benmarl were thriving. They would produce their first small vintage this autumn. The grapes we used for wine-making at this point were those from our Hartsdale vineyard and the various old experimental varieties developed by Mr. Caywood based on the Delaware grape, which abounded on the farm. Our optimism was further confirmed by the excellent wines being made by Everett Crosby at his High Tor vineyard in nearby Rockland County. We applied for research grants wherever we could. No luck.

If only we could sell our wine. There was no question about its being well liked. Friends, local restaurants, and a few of the more sophisticated stores could easily help us dispose of the small amounts we made, and the revenues from these sales could at least pay Milton's salary and meet a part of the cost of operations. Actually there was nothing to prevent me from obtaining a license to do just this—except the cost. There was no charge for a federal license. The hitch was that the state of New York charged a rather high license fee, plus fees for label registration and so on. The total costs of all permits, bonds, and other fees I calculated were very nearly $1,600 a year. The proceeds from at least four of the approximately five acres we were cultivating would be required to go to these expenses. The remaining net earnings would not come close to covering operating costs.

Everett Crosby and I had discussed this problem. A lower license cost, we thought, might help matters. It would certainly be helpful to us and in addition it just might lure other people into growing wine grapes. In spite of the success Everett and I had met with, we could both see that, if there was ever to be a renaissance of the early Hudson Valley grape-growing industry as a supplier of wine, a great deal more research was needed than we could provide. He had tried to organize some political effort to modify the State Liquor Authority regulations in his area of Rockland County but so far had not accomplished much.

I approached my local state senator, Clinton Dominic,

who lived in Newburgh nearby. He agreed to help try to obtain legislation to lower license fees if I could demonstrate support for the plan. I then approached Dale Swartzmiller, who ran the regional office of the State Chamber of Commerce, and persuaded him that lower fees would have a salutary effect on our chronically depressed local agricultural economy. There were many farmers in our area who knew how to make wine. Many of them earned a high proportion of their living selling farm produce from roadside stands. If a wine license were cheap there would be no reason why they couldn't make and sell good fresh country wines along with jellies, fruit, and vegetables. Dale gave me tremendous cooperation, introducing me to dozens of potentially interested farmers. We drafted a statement of suggested legislative modifications and started collecting names on a petition to support it.

Together we drove to Albany to let me appeal directly to the State Commissioner of Agriculture for his assistance. The commissioner was sympathetic but realistically pointed out that the most effective source of the kind of support we needed to obtain legislative reform would have to come from the large number of grape farmers in the Finger Lakes region of western New York State, who supplied the grapes for the major New York wineries, such as the Taylor Wine Company, Widmer's, and Gold Seal. Most of these farmers belonged to an organization called the New York Grape Growers Association. I wrote to a local chapter, whose head forwarded my appeal for support to the president of the parent organization. He thought that my plan for lowering license fees would be regarded by the Grape Growers' most important clients, the big wineries, as a source of eventual competition and he feared that they would take punitive action against his organization if it supported me. "Don't rock the boat" was his reply.

Senator Dominic, nonetheless, helped us redraft and present our plea for reform in the state legislature. Our bill never got out of the committee assigned to consider it. Finally, Dominic told me that, just as the western New York growers had suspected, the large wineries opposed the idea and their political strength was sufficient to quash my idea with not much more effort than a frown. "Taylor," meaning the Taylor Wine Company, "said to forget it," said Dominic. "Unless you have a fortune to spend organizing support," he went on, "my only advice would also have to be: forget it."

Under the stress of my financial circumstances there was nothing more that I could do—then. But I certainly couldn't "forget it." The opportunity to revive my efforts would come again.

Dene decided to find a job until our financial situation improved. She was an excellent draftsman, having worked in the design division of aircraft factories before America entered World War II, then, after we had married, in post engineers' offices during the war while camp-following me from post to post. Her really outstanding talent, though, had emerged when, just after the war, she had worked in a major architect's office in Los Angeles and become a superb designer. She found a job with a Poughkeepsie firm, where her talent and warm, cooperative personality won her quick respect.

When I could be home for a few days Milton and I worked intensely in the vineyards. Besides the regular maintenance work in the Delawares which Milton did alone, there was tractor work that only I could do. The new French wine grapes grew rapidly, particularly the Baco Noir and the Seyval Blanc, which at that time was more often referred to as Seyve-Villard 5276. The Chardonnay was also extremely vigorous. To support the young vines temporarily, each trunk was trained erect by tying it to a stake split from the old rot-shortened posts we had recovered from the discarded vineyards. As fast as possible we built the permanent trellises for these vines. The longer of the old recovered posts were distributed along the rows. Then, carrying my step stool; a twelve-pound maul; the fifteen-pound podger, which was still the best post-setting tool we had been able to find for our shaly land; a short-handled axe to resharpen posts; a pruning saw to square off the striking ends of damaged posts; and a carpenter's apron full of number-ten nails (which we preferred to staples), I labored doggedly up one row and down another. I would podge a hole between every two or three vines, set and pound in a post, then drive in two nails to carry the trellis wire. It was just too much trouble to carry one more tool to measure each post for nail placement, so we devised an adequate quick system: "top nail, nipple high—bottom nail, belly low," and sang it to ourselves to a tune from *South Pacific.* It was hard, hand-blistering, backbreaking, mind-numbing work, and I fell into bed at night aching in every muscle and joint, but somehow grateful that it hurt. I damn well deserved it for letting the farm get us into such a fix.

We scheduled the picking party for the 10th of September. On a whimsical impulse one morning in my New York studio, I telephoned the *New York Times* and the New York *Daily News.* Both agreed to cover the event. The response from our friends to help us pick was almost overwhelming. Everyone who was asked agreed to come and "could they please bring a friend?" Dene, the boys, Milton, and I threw ourselves into preparation. We built more picnic tables and cleaned picking baskets. There weren't enough bushel baskets for the hordes we expected, so we dug out of the barn a hundred or more of the century-old handmade trugs fitted with grapevine handles. They were light and would be easy for the youngsters and our urban friends to manage. The winemaking equipment was scrubbed, the vineyards harrowed then bladed smooth even though we normally let weeds and grass grow this time of year to compete with the vines, encouraging early ripening of fruit and dormancy of the vine wood. If we were going to have our picture in the *Times* and *Daily News* we had to look spiffy.

To discourage birds from eating the ripening grapes I had devised a number of "scarers," which we distributed over the farm. Eight-foot sections of used tin pipe were mounted on tall poles. A length of upholsterer's beading cord which had been soaked in saltpeter was hung inside the tubing. The fuses of cherry-bomb firecrackers were inserted between the strands of the soaked beading. When ignited at the bottom, the beading would burn slowly upward, igniting the fuses of the firecrackers, which dropped into a pan at the bottom of the tube and burst at intermittent intervals. The irregularly-timed explosions upset the birds and minimized their damage to the grapes. I would eventually discover that commercially-built cannons were available, but at the time my own invention worked well enough. We loaded them all. Even though bird damage was minimal at the time, I thought the constant explosions would lend a bit of excitement to the day's activities.

The most eager of our guests began to arrive early Saturday morning. By noon the five-acre area around the farm buildings was filled with cars and the vineyards literally swarming with bright-colored, expensively-dressed amateur grape pickers, including the New York State Commissioner of Agriculture and all of our old Hartsdale neighbors, who had helped us in the past and now served as "crew chiefs" to show our hundreds of milling *vendangeurs* how to pick grapes.

Kim, now an expert tractor driver at the age of 12, organized the guests' children into basket-gathering platoons, piled the grape-filled bushels and trugs onto a trailer and hauled them to the barn for processing. We had hundreds more hands than we needed so Milton put them to work sorting out the ripest grapes to make what he called a *"bearinoutslaysem"* wine (after the German *beerenauslese*). In spite of a crop of a number of tons more than we had ever had in the past it was soon all picked. We formed a long line to the de-stemmer we had borrowed from Everett Crosby, so that each picker could toss a ritual basket into the machine. Everyone was conscious of the presence of the newspaper photographers.

Someone had the idea of enthroning a king and queen of the harvest. Among the dozens of deft artists' hands a pair of Bacchic crowns woven of vine shoots, leaves, and grapes were made. A pair of "leopard" car blankets became animal-skin robes, and two of the guests were chosen as the royal couple. Then, festooned with their makeshift costumes, they were lifted into a large vat of grapes and cheered wildly as they "treaded" out the symbolic first flow of the *vendange.* It was all foolish, farcical fun.

Dene and helpers had literally piled the big tables with a fabulous buffet of casseroles, fresh grapes, apples, and pumpkins. There were more drinkers than there was wine from the previous harvest, so when it ran out, twenty-gallon crocks were filled with a punch made from every alcoholic beverage I could find in my cellar. No one seemed to mind. We set up a keg of fresh cider for the children. Again our revelers stayed until the chill of the September evening overcame the warmth of wine and finally the last car was gone.

The next day we were famous! The telephone began to ring at nine o'clock and didn't stop. "You're in today's *Daily News!*" We frantically began to try to find a newsdealer in Marlboro who carried the paper. No success. Finally we found one in Newburgh with a single copy left and dashed down to buy it. It was true. Two full pages of beautiful photography with a nice story about the day's festivities. Nothing so grand as this had even been dreamed of!

Monday morning's mail included the first trickle of what eventually became a flood of hundreds of congratulatory or inquiring letters. Then the phone began to ring again. "You're in the *New York Times!*" Another miracle! On the front page of the second section I read myself being quoted: "When I think of all the fine wines I could have in my cellar if I hadn't started making my own . . ." In spite of the intoxicating excitement, the irony of that quote shot a momentary fantasy of fear searing through me. Dene would find reinforcement in it for her doubts about our new life.

I answered every letter: "Yes, please do feel free to come and see the farm."—"No, unfortunately we cannot send you wine; we are not licensed to sell." On the day following the *New York Times* story, two rather somber-looking men drove up and asked to see "Mr. Miller." "I'm sorry, but we have sold out of grapes," I said with a smile, acknowledging that I was Miller and assuming that they were home winemakers. One of the men opened a small wallet showing an identification card. "Internal Revenue," he said. "Could we see your winemaking facilities?" Sobering immediately, I led them to the barn. They looked, without speaking, at everything, thumped the barrels and asked me to remove the water valve which allowed the CO_2 to escape and also kept insects out. One of them sniffed the open bung. "I have my householder's permit," I said. "May we see it?" I pointed to it, tacked on the wall.

"Come here," he said, walking over to it. "How many people did you have here on Saturday?"

"Oh, about two hundred."

"Read that sentence," he said.

I knew it forbade the householder to sell, give away, or make wine for anyone other than his family.

"But these were all our personal guests—friends," I said, flushing with embarrassed disbelief.

"I have a report that you were seen taking money from someone."

"But that was a home winemaker who came to buy grapes!"

"What's his name?"

"Well, if it was Saturday morning," I said, "his name was Ken MacLeish. He works for *Fortune* magazine and his father is the Librarian of Congress."

The man rubbed his chin a minute, looked at his companion, and took out his handkerchief and blew his nose.

They both stood silently for what seemed a long time to me, hands in their pockets, running their eyes once more over everything.

"Well," one said, "we have to check these things out, you know." At last they seemed completely reassured and their manner became friendly as we walked to their car and drove away.

Winter came early but it didn't matter. This year we were well finished with our summer work, the new vineyards harrowed, trellised, the young vines well trained, their trunks ramrod straight. I began, thankfully, to get some decently well-paying painting work to do, so I stayed in town for long periods. Milton could manage the necessary chores alone.

One snowy morning, when I had had to catch an early train to deliver a job to *Saturday Evening Post* in the city, I drove out across the path Milton had already shoveled for the car from the garage to the highway. As I passed him and waved, he looked "fit and fine," but by evening he had taken to his bed exhausted. Thank heavens we had completed the renovation of his house. He could be ill in comfort. He was tended by a "housekeeper," who occasionally looked after him, one of a series he had kept during the years. She summoned us early, a morning or two later, worried. Milton was perceptibly worse. We called a doctor, who called an ambulance and took him to the hospital. "It is his heart," the doctor said. He stayed comatose for a few days and then died. Through friends we located a few relatives. We arranged a quiet funeral. No one knew of any religious affiliation he might have had, so his service was composed of testimonials by all of us who had known the fine old man. We laid him to rest in a nearby cemetery, where his nephew said he thought Milton would like to stay.

The farm seemed empty without my old companion. As I went about the place I was reminded of him in many ways. I had taken out the tractor's battery and was blocking its wheels up to keep the weight off the tires and checked myself as I was about to put a bigger block on top of a small one. I had done that before, disastrously. Milton and I had been repairing the rotten barn sills. We had lifted the corner of the building and I was placing temporary blocks when one, off-balance, turned and the entire weight of the barn fell on my forefinger. Blood spurted from it. Milton saw what had happened and almost turned white. The finger didn't hurt although it appeared to be mashed flat. "I'll have to learn to draw with my feet," I thought, waiting for Milton to hurriedly find a length of pipe to lever the weight off so that I could withdraw my hand. We rushed off to the emergency room of the hospital. Luckily the damage was insignificant. My finger had been caught under a rotted portion of wood, which had cushioned the weight and saved the bone from being crushed. In a few days the finger was back in use. "Don't ever do that to me again!" he admonished, wiping his forehead with his red bandana.

Other memories came to mind. Once I had made the mistake of referring to his housekeeper as his wife: "Wife? No sir. She ain't no woman of mine either by marriage or farmication!" I smiled, thinking of his pride in the fact that no matter how boldly he pulled it out of the ground by hand he was immune to poison "ivory." Although most of his personal belongings had been taken by his nephew or given away, I came across his old brandy still, a rusty shotgun, and a handleless .22 rifle he planned to fix. I put them away in the attic of the gate cottage which had been his house.

Not long after Milton's death the European clients I had found on my first trip abroad became increasingly important, and after careful thought and a visit to England and the continent I made the momentous decision to move to Europe. I couldn't allow myself to think about what would happen to my farm. My one hope of finding a way to keep it going, Milton, was now gone. As I had learned earlier, it would be difficult to find a buyer for the farm who would pay enough for it. It would take a while. A local real-estate broker had agreed to serve as a renting agent in the meantime and find a tenant after we had gone. We would refurbish Milton's gate cottage with a bedroom and studio that I could use when I came back to see the farm from time to time.

The grapes were nearly ripe but I would not make any wine this year. Perhaps never again. Home winemakers would come in next week to pick the grapes after Dene and the boys sailed tomorrow on the *Queen Elizabeth* for their new home. I would stay on a bit longer. I moved the wine press and the small hand-operated crusher into the cellar portion of the barn winery, which could be locked more securely than the outer shed. There were two barrels of wine from last year's harvest on their racks, surrounded by a half-dozen glass carboys. From habit, I thought, "Must get back to rack them at least once before spring." The racking and transfer hoses were coiled neatly and hung on the wall. "What a sweet ill-fated little winery!"

I put away a bronze bas-relief casting of a centaur I had modeled from clay, intending eventually to finish it as a weather vane, laying it in the dark-stained ornately carved buffet that I had impulsively bought at an auction, only to find that Dene wouldn't have the monster in her house. The boys and I nicknamed it the "Black Maria," and it had become the catch-all cabinet for small winery supplies. Beside it on the shelf was a plaster model of another decoration I had modeled for the winery door, an escutcheon with the Marlborough family crest of a cross and rampant lion in two of its quarters and clusters of grapes in the other two. A partially filled wine glass was in the center. Beneath the shield I had fashioned a ribbon with the motto, "In Vino Veritas." Well, truth for some perhaps; for me I might better have made it read, "In wine, misery." I was feeling very sorry for myself.

The next afternoon, after the massive steamer had pulled away from the dock and I could no longer see Dene's figure at the railing, I drove home to the farm. I put away the car and walked slowly up the hill toward the place where

I had first fallen under the spell of Benmarl. The sun was low, just behind the trees that edged the bluff at the property's western boundary. As I stood looking down across the valley the sun threw my shadow grotesquely across the terraced vines, plunging its elongated shape down toward the farmhouse like an accusing finger. "No use accusing the farm," I thought, defending it. If there was blame to be placed it would have to be on me. This old hill had her own destiny to fulfill. Mutely, by inspiration, she had tried to make me the instrument of that fulfillment, but I just hadn't been big enough for the job. She would try again, I was sure. She had done well with Andrew Caywood. The imprint of his labors was still apparent. They had reached across more than a century to inspire me that first day I had stood here. I hadn't managed to build my château as I had planned, but at least I had arrested the slow deterioration of his work. There would be someone else to carry on. Perhaps my real-estate broker would bring some young, stronger man to stand here as Mr. Wardell had brought me, and Benmarl would show him her valley and make him see it filled with wine vines, and he would succeed.

chapter VI

The Burgundy Years

Finding a pleasant house to rent in a region where there is very little transient population is always quite a feat, but Dene managed it with characteristic resourcefulness. She wrote the Office de Tourisme in Beaune and received a prompt reply from a Monsieur Desangle, who informed us that there were seldom rentals available except for summer occupancy, but that he happened to know of a house of reasonable size and comfort in a remote little wine village called St. Romain, to the southwest of Beaune. We made arrangements to drive down to see the house with some misgivings. Although a good French school for the boys was not a consideration—we had decided on English boarding schools for them—an isolated village we'd never heard of that we could not even find on our maps was not exactly what we'd had in mind, and we'd had dreams of having a famous address like Chambertin or Nuits-St.-Georges. It didn't take long to dispel our fears. We drove from Beaune with Monsieur Desangle down a beautiful tree-lined road to the south and turned off the main road through the vineyards of Pommard. The immaculate vines, deep green against a red-brown soil, seemed to stretch in every direction as far as we could see, and we were shortly in Volnay with no break in the sea of vines. At this point we had risen quite high on the Côte, and as we looked off to the east toward Switzerland we had a lovely panoramic view of the Jura Mountains.

We skirted Meursault to the north and passed through two lesser wine villages, each as fantastically picturesque as the other. By the time we reached the first road sign pointing to St. Romain it hardly mattered what it would be like. We'd already seen what we had hoped to find. Even so, nothing could really have prepared us for St. Romain itself. Its setting is breathtaking. The village is built in two parts on a hill, standing steeply, from our view, like the prow of a gigantic stone ship sailing the floor of a crater, surrounded by miles of steep palisadelike cliffs. At the top of the hill, amid the ruins of an ancient castle, stood St. Romain le haut.

Nestling tranquilly in its valley is St. Romain le bas. Its stone buildings ringing the base of the hill stacked themselves gently up the slopes, creating the illusion of a medieval stage setting in a vast amphitheater. There was no one in sight. We felt as if we should whisper as our car climbed slowly through the ancient streets.

The first glimpse of our proposed residence was framed by a pair of huge ornate wrought-iron gates. It was a large stone house surrounded by numerous outbuildings forming a rear courtyard, all enclosed by a massive stone wall, situated on the village square between the only hotel in town and the *mairie,* or town hall. In spite of its size, the residence itself was a simple, dignified rectangular building with a black slate roof. A brass *dentale* ran along the ridge, and there was a weather vane creaking in a slight breeze. Unlike most of the neighboring buildings, it had been whitewashed and stood out sharply against the dark vineyards rising to the palisades behind it. Tall shuttered windows were spaced evenly across its façade. Its only pretension was a false portico, which vaguely suggested that its designer had wished to create the impression of a small château. Two steps rose to a small entry terrace; its thick slabs of stone were full of fossilized coral, which we later found in abundance everywhere in the valley.

The house was completely furnished, albeit in a way strange to us. There was no parlor or living room. When I asked where one entertained guests, I was told, "Mais dans la salle à manger, monsieur!" Where else indeed but the dining room in a Burgundian *maison de la campagne.* Besides the dining room there was a large kitchen with a wood-burning cookstove and a pantry. There was a small library or study and upstairs there were four bedrooms. Oh yes, tucked away behind the stairs was a small bathroom. This was to be the extent of our living quarters, although there was much more to the house. A large attic and many other rooms were all piled with old furniture and closed off.

That evening we returned to Beaune, to the Hôtel de la Poste, where we were staying. The Petitjeans' house was interesting, we both agreed, but Dene was worried about it. "Imagine having no drawing room!" There was also no central heating. The upstairs bedrooms' fireplaces were sealed, and one depended entirely on warmth rising from the first floor, heated by the large kitchen stove and another small decorated ceramic stove in the dining room. Not much different from the way we originally found Benmarl, I realized.

The next morning I called Monsieur Desangle to say that we would like to see the St. Romain house again. A few hours later we met him at his office in the Bureau de Tourisme in Beaune. He told us Madame Petitjean, the owner, wanted to meet us and would accompany us to see the house. We picked her up at her Beaune house and retraced our previous drive.

As we approached St. Romain she volunteered occasional explanatory remarks about the passing landscape. We approached a large sign almost as big as an American billboard. "St. Romain, mon village," it said. There was a drawing of a knight in armor, sword drawn, charging on a rampant horse. As if the sign were a painting, the signature "Roland Thévenin" appeared at the lower left corner. Madame Petitjean smiled when I asked about it.

"Monsieur Thévenin est le maire de St. Romain," she said. This opened a flood of discussion about him between her and Monsieur Desangle, in French too rapid and colloquial for me to follow. "He's doing well, I suppose?" asked Desangle at last. Madame pursed her lips, drawing air in softly, lifted her eyes skyward for an instant and dangled her hand limply back and forth. "Il est confortable," she said in what was obviously intended as a gross understatement. She pointed to a small but very handsome château we were passing on the left. Monsieur Thévenin had given it to his first wife to smooth the way for a second marriage. We passed a long row of walled buildings on the right. "His cellars. Also that row on the left." His private business offices were on the right again, in the lower floors of his mother, Madame Buonaterra's, home. The curiosity that was growing in my mind about this man was further aroused when Monsieur Desangle said, "You will like Maire Thévenin; he is a great man, a poet, with a great heart."

Just ahead was the *mairie,* and next to it, separated by a tall stone wall was Madame's house. Monsieur Desangle parked in front of the gates and we entered the courtyard through a small iron door in the wall to the left of the large gates. Madame Petitjean removed from her bag the large key Monsieur Desangle had used before and opened the door, but instead of walking in, she bent over to remove her shoes and stepped into a pair of felt slippers. Monsieur Desangle followed suit, and as there were more slippers, Dene and I did the same. We would later discover the reason for this unfamiliar custom. The slippers were the removable linings of wooden *sabots,* which were commonly worn in rural Burgundy for vineyard work. In order to keep from tracking in mud, one left the outside footgear at the door and retained the liners for house wear.

Madame Petitjean showed us everything we had seen

before, but this time the queer old furnishings somehow took on a different look as she spoke of her life here. She had grown up in this house. She had been born in that bed. She took us into the west wing of the house through a very large room stuffed with more old furniture, paintings, and photographs. This had been the ballroom, she said, when she was a girl. The playroom had been there. A maid's room here. Gradually, we began to see the place as it must have been in earlier days, a comfortable country home of a somewhat more-affluent-than-average Burgundian family.

There was a front courtyard and a rear courtyard. In the rear courtyard was a stone trough fed by a big old hand pump, where the weekly wash was done. Across the rear court were two stone barns, and behind one of these was a very pleasant kitchen garden with espaliered grapevines growing on the high walls surrounding it. Underneath the whole complex of courts and buildings was a huge wine cellar, all in stone with Roman arched ceilings. This was not to be part of our rental, as it was already rented to a firm of wine *négociants* in Beaune, who aged a portion of their Pommard and Volnay wines in it. We were warned not to be alarmed when their men came to *faire plein* (top up) the barrels. Indeed, we learned not only not to be alarmed but also to be always present when their men came, as we were permitted on these occasions to watch the work and also to taste great vintages we might never otherwise have known.

Later, when we were presented to Roland Thévenin, the mayor, we didn't perceive immediately how much more he was than the political head of the village. After a while we came to realize that he and his family were its first citizens in many ways. Besides being a major landholder he was the *négociant* through whom almost all the wine produced in local vineyards was sold. He purchased young wine from local growers, blended it, aged it, and bottled it for shipment to market. Because of his untiring insistence on the outstanding merit of its wines, the village had been granted the right to the appellation of origin, "St. Romain." Thus its wines were now marketed for their own distinctive characteristics, whereas before they had been sold anonymously for much less favorable prices and marketed as ordinary Burgundy wine. In addition, the enterprising mayor even traveled to America to find a market for the produce of his village. His talents were not limited to business and politics. He was also an excellent poet, a published author, and a member of the Académie des Lettres of the University of Dijon. In all his capacities he sang constantly of the beauties and virtues of his little fiefdom, which the sign had aptly referred to as "mon village."

Monsieur Thévenin received us warmly. He liked *les américains* and considered it a compliment that we had gone to the trouble to learn his language; he was "honored" to have us come to live in his village. The following morning a messenger delivered a formal note from the mayor's mother, Madame Buonaterra, requesting that Monsieur and Madame Miller join her, the *maire* and his family, for a "Kir" which would be poured in our honor at her home at four o'clock. Madame Buonaterra was virtually the queen mother of St. Romain and this invitation was not merely to say "please stop by for a drink and a chat." This was to be, in Burgundian tradition, our proper welcome to the village.

The custom of the Kir was begun by the Chanoine Kir, mayor of the ancient Burgundian capital city of Dijon. Monsieur Kir, as his title indicated, was, in addition to being the mayor of his city, a canon of the church in his region. He was also honored for his part in the Resistance during World War II. His great love for the *bons* of his native Burgundy and his success in bringing them to the attention of the rest of the country had earned for him great respect, and at the age of eighty-seven he was almost a legendary figure throughout France. It was his habit to serve those who called on him at his office a glass of good white Burgundy wine with a large splash of another fine regional product, the rich deep red syrup of the black currant, crème de cassis. This delicious cordial had become a symbol of formal hospitality in

Burgundy, and an invitation for a Kir carried with it a rather special flavor of official welcome.

During the course of a year in St. Romain, there are, as we soon learned, many official celebrations in which all the townspeople participate, and we were invited to every town function. One of the things we noticed was that wine was always an important part of every event. The ceremonies are brief and all pretty much conducted in the same manner. For example on Armistice Day the villagers gather in front of the *mairie,* the veterans stand in a group to one side, the honor guard (volunteer firemen in shining brass helmets) and members of the horn and drum corps on the other. A roll of drums, a fanfare by the horns, a few words from the mayor, a wreath laid at the foot of the memorial, a silent prayer, and a chorus of "La Marseillaise" by the school children grouped on the steps, then the horns and drums signal the end. It is very simple yet very moving.

Immediately afterward a *vin d'honneur* is held in the *salle des fêtes* at the rear of the *mairie.* It is a large room and its long banquet table is draped with white. On it are dozens of wine glasses standing shoulder to shoulder, an open bottle of St. Romain *blanc* inserted about every six glasses. The wine is poured, glasses are lifted, the mayor toasts the martyrs, everyone sips in unison, and the official ceremony is finished.

I don't remember seeing any nondrinkers except the very young. After the ceremony all are welcome to stay and drink and chat informally. No one stays too long and no one uses it as an opportunity for serious drinking. We will always remember our first attendance at one of these occasions. After the ceremonies had ended and we had just sipped the *vin d'honneur* the mayor offered another toast, "Aux premières citoyens américains de St. Romain," and over a hundred glasses of wine were raised in our honor.

In January of our first year St. Romain was to take its turn as host for the great Fête de St. Vincent. It is a supreme honor to be given such an enormous responsibility. St. Vincent is the patron of the *vigneron,* and on his day each year the attention of all France focuses on which ever Burgundian village is serving as host. Preparation went on for months. Notable personalities flowed through the *mairie* and *vins d'honneur* began to account for more wine consumption in our household than mealtimes.

One mild afternoon I had installed myself in a sunny spot on the terrace, carving a decorative cluster of grapes on a piece of stone, when two strangers passed our open gates. One man glanced in and, seeing me chipping away at my stone, he clapped his hand upon his companion's sleeve and with a sharp intake of breath, as if he had seen something startling, said in a loud stage whisper, "Attend! Qu'est-ce que c'est?"

"Où?"

"Shh, la bas, un sculpteur . . ."

"Ahhhhhhh."

I looked up, smiled briefly and bent again over my work. I didn't wish to start a conversation. For one thing, I am not a stone sculptor and I was quite self-conscious about the fact that I didn't really know how to handle the unfamiliar tools I had about me, and also I felt the design I had begun was trivial. The visitors, however, were not to be put off. They had undoubtedly come to the village of the ebullient Maire Thévenin prepared to find a veritable living museum of ancient buildings, lifestyles, and crafts. I was wearing a dusty beret and an old leather *tonnelier*'s apron loaned to me by our cook's husband, Monsieur Jacquet. They had mistaken me for a local artisan, plying his ancient trade, which had undoubtedly been handed down from father to son for generations. I could almost feel this idea crystallize in their minds as they tiptoed diffidently toward me. I smiled again and murmured, "Bonjour." I didn't want to appear rude. They might be important guests of the *maire*.

"Continuez, monsieur." "Don't let us disturb you," one said heartily and, in a loud whisper to the other, "Ahh, regardez, a cluster of grapes," as he saw the subject of my work.

To me: "The famous grapes of Burgundy, eh, monsieur?"

"Oui, monsieur," I replied, embarrassed.

"To be recorded for posterity, eh?" he went on. In a few moments they had built up such a romantic idea of my role in the ancient culture that I hated to disappoint them. I tapped away even more intently, answering their questions as often as possible with only a smile or a nod, realizing if I spoke more than a word or two they would detect my American accent immediately and the illusion they had constructed would be shattered. After a while they tiptoed away with much bowing and smiling and tipping of hats. "Au 'voir, monsieur." Shortly, the bell on the small gate tinkled and Maire Thévenin rushed in doubled up in laughter. The two men, representatives of a Brussels newspaper, who had come for a briefing on the St. Vincent *fête*, had arrived at his office delighted with their quaint experience. He too had been unable to disabuse them of their agreeable illusion. We lifted our glasses and Monsieur Thévenin said, "To St. Romain, et ses ancien artisans!"

In preparation for the Fête de St. Vincent, almost all the women in the village were busy in their spare time weaving garlands of evergreen branches and making paper flowers and other decorations which would be used to festoon the village streets on the day of the celebration. The wives of several of Monsieur Thévenin's employees also took part in these activities, and Dene was delighted to be included.

I was able to spend a pleasant few weeks with our Burgundian friends, visiting their vineyards and cellars, drinking their wines with them. Although we had met the great Latour family of winegrowers and shippers on earlier visits, Mark Chevillot and Roland Thévenin now introduced us to many other prominent growers and *négociants*—Drouhin, the Bouchards, Noëllat, Faiveley, the Compt de Vogüé, Madame Leroy, the Ropiteaus, and dozens of others.

I enjoyed these visits to great and famous properties very much. I was fascinated to discover that none of them operated in exactly the same manner; each reflected the varied attitudes and philosophies of their proprietors. I felt a strong empathy with them. They were artists, I told myself. And, just as two artists of different taste and character may take the same tools and materials and work from the same subject, they will invariably add a third ingredient (their own subjective point of view) and their results will be significantly and interestingly different. This is true, as I was learning, of winemaking. They were remarkably open with me. There was never a feeling that any secret technique was being withheld. To the contrary, when they learned that I grew and made wine myself they went to great lengths to show me in the most minute detail their winemaking equipment and their vineyard tools. We deplored together the difficulties of obtaining good corks, the high cost of bottles, the frustrations of weather, the manner of and reasons for different vineyard management, and, of course, the difficulties of marketing—the bottom line.

On this last subject I had almost nothing to contribute from experience, but I found that my views about the tastes of my countrymen were of great consequence to them anyway. It seemed that the whole wine world understood that the people of the vast continent of North America, and especially the affluent United States, were just beginning to enjoy and drink wine as a part of their meals. The success or failure to attract that developing market was a matter of vital importance. Most of those I discussed this subject with were well-to-do, sophisticated, well-traveled people. They knew as well as I did that wine was still only a minor part of American cuisine. In the early 1960s Americans drank less than two gallons of wine per capita per year, whereas in Europe the consumption rate averaged from twenty-five to thirty-five gallons per capita. United States liquor stores (very few called themselves "wine shops" at that time) usually displayed wine only on a few shelves in the back parts of their establishments. The rest of their stock consisted of whiskey and other beverages of higher alcoholic content, less subtle than table wine and not ordinarily used, or appropriate for, service with food.

I enjoyed my role as consultant and unappointed testifier to the attitudes and underlying motivations of my vast and mysteriously wine-resistant people. The truth is I learned a lot more than I taught. I frankly hadn't ever thought a great deal about my countrymen's drinking habits or attitudes. Now I found it fascinating to drink the varied and magnificent wines of Burgundy, and eat the magnificent food of Burgundy, and speculate with the prominent producers of Burgundy as to whether or not larger quantities of the wine of Burgundy could be sold to Americans. Luckily, alcohol has never made me loquacious. The less I talked the more wine was poured. The less I talked the more I heard what were probably very wise assessments of the American wine market, which (although I didn't know it then) I would be trying to enter with my own wines in a few years' time.

I deeply appreciated being made privy to the thoughts and philosophies of these people, who, in my opinion, made the greatest wines in the world, both the great and the small among them. But I have to confess that I enjoyed most of all the privilege of being accepted by the smaller ones. Among them our relationship was focused on the kind of matters I was used to dealing with at Benmarl, the day-today problems of vineyard operation, the actual handling of, and decision making about, the wine during the many stages it goes through. Some did everything the way their fathers and grandfathers had always done it; some were trying new techniques. It was among this latter group that I felt most comfortable.

For me this was a period of intensive learning although I didn't realize it at the time. I had such a limited background in winemaking myself that I wasn't conscious of the differences in the techniques that I was observing from those used, say, in California. Neither, apparently, were most of the young Burgundians, many of whom had never been away from their own milieu. It would not be until I returned to my own vineyard and winemaking that I would become aware of the often subtle but important differences between the Burgundian practices and those that were common in America. For example, small new oak cooperage, usually made from oak of the Nevers region, gives a pleasant astringency to the young wines, which would eventually in later years become a part of the complex toasted flavor unique to mature Côte d'Or burgundies.

It seems strange today but less than ten years ago most American winemakers took elaborate precautions to prevent the conversion of the malic acids in their wines to the softer-tasting lactic acid. This malo-lactic fermentation, as it is called, was often considered in America to be undesirable because if improperly managed it can result in bad flavors. In Burgundy it was recognized as essential, and the correct management of it was almost instinctively a part of their winemaking practices. The conversion is carried out by special microorganisms, just as the alcoholic fermentation is carried out by the yeast. These bacteria are apparently indigenous to most old-world wine regions, and they spontaneously go about their important work in Burgundy when the winemakers provide the necessary conditions for them to develop in their wines. When I tried to do the same, later in America, I discovered that I could not obtain a spontaneous

malic conversion and eventually had to order a culture of the bacteria from France to initiate their development at Benmarl.

These young Burgundians, I found, rarely changed anything very drastically. After all, a few centuries of trial and error had resulted in a very dependable *modus operandi.* But they wanted to know *why* things happened the way they did. Most of them were graduates of the oenological school in Beaune and had carried their education in winemaking to just about the limits possible within the state of the art at that time.

One young man in particular, Henri Latour, from the nearby village of Auxey-Duresses became a good friend. He had been introduced to us by Madame Petitjean, who recommended his wine as the "best of the local growers." He also made the estate wines from the Petitjean vineyards. Henri subscribed to wine technology magazines from all over the world and admired the advances that were being made in the United States. He was aware of the development of the first automatic grape-harvesting machines, which was then taking place in New York. He was also aware of the research work of Dr. Nelson Shaulis of New York's Geneva Agricultural Experiment Station regarding the relationship of the size of the grapevine's leaf curtain to the amount of crop the vine was able to ripen. He was testing Dr. Shaulis's theory, in fact, by training one of his vineyards onto a six-foot-high trellis in contrast to the normal three-foot style employed generally in the Côte d'Or.

He was familiar with the hybrid vine varieties I was growing at Benmarl, particularly with the one known as Baco No. 1. There were large areas of this variety being grown on the eastern side of the Route Nationale 74 in the *lieux-dits*, having the right to identify area wines as "Bourgogne" but having no communal identification. The Baco vines were being gradually removed and replaced with Pinot Noir or other varieties historically identified with the Côte d'Or region. This was required in order for their growers to retain the appellation of origin identification, which had high market value. These growers resented the necessity of removing the Baco vines because they were much hardier and more productive than the required replacement and, in the opinion of many, produced a better wine in those areas. The real reason, they claimed, was *politique* or, more to the point, *économique.* The Baco vine made an excellent wine which could be sold cheaper than those of many of their more politically powerful neighbors on the west side of Nationale 74.

I asked Henri what he thought of their claims. This rather put him on the spot, because his wines were qualified to carry a much more highly regarded appellation, and in a sense he was one of those whose common interests would be served by putting the Baco down. Nonetheless, his reply was that, if the Baco growers could afford to produce their wines with the same expensive care given to the *grands vins,* they would truly be able to compete among the best wines of the region.

The first *vendange,* or harvest, while we were residents of

a Burgundian village resides in my memory as a collage of oddly blended vignettes and images of old and familiar situations in a bizarre new setting. The quiet intensity in the ruddy faces of farming people as they wait the last suspenseful days before harvest is much the same in a small Oklahoma cotton town as in a wine village in Burgundy. A kind of grim tension seems to set the jaw. Conversation becomes terse. Eyes glance nervously at the sky. *La grêle* is a dreaded scourge in the Côte d'Or.

I understood well the anxiety in the faces of our new neighbors. Hail had also been a dreaded scourge in Eldorado, Oklahoma. I remembered from boyhood Tommy Aiken's mahogany face, skin cracked like a drought-parched mud flat, glowering with squinted eyes at a black cloud looming across his field. He switched a cud of chewing tobacco to the other cheek and spat a stream of brown juice defiantly. Suddenly egg-sized hailstones drove us to shelter on his rickety planked porch, and drummed thunderously on its tin roof. As suddenly, it stopped and the entire scene burst into brilliant red-gold as the light of a setting sun broke through the clouds. Tommy walked ahead of me toward his ruined crop, kicking aside the inches of hailstones as he stared down at the broken plants, their bolls of soft cotton beaten into the sandy red dirt. He took off his broad-brimmed sweat-stained hat and wiped his forehead with a large ragged handkerchief. His brow, sheltered by his hat, was pale in contrast to his deeply burned face. "Damn!" he murmured helplessly. The bank owned him for another year.

Tommy would have loved the French way of combating hail that prevailed at the time. Into the sky they fired mortarlike explosives, which burst in the threatening clouds, theoretically breaking up the particles of falling ice crystals, interfering with their accumulation into lumps big enough to damage the ripening grapes. Whether it worked or not, the feeling of fighting back, instead of helplessly awaiting one's fate at the hands of an indifferent nature, must have provided great satisfaction.

Another advantage enjoyed, it seemed to me, by my Burgundian farmer friends, over those vividly remembered prairie farmers of my youth, was the fact that here a large part of the responsibility for success or failure was placed in the hands of highly specialized heavenly protectors, such as, for example, St. Vincent, whose legendary weakness for wine made him especially attentive to winemakers. Our village also paid homage to another even more specialized patron, St. Grégoire, whose duty it was to arrange for a good harvest. The town crier, ringing his bell for attention, announced his day on the fifth of September. The elements of this celebration were always essentially the same—a parade, a speech, perhaps a testimonial of thanks for a past success, always concluded by an occasion to break bread and share a glass of wine with one's fellows. Whether or not the intercession of this heavenly lobbying system always produced the hoped-for results, a comforting sense of a shared common weal was renewed with each event.

I didn't see or hear of any hail damage that year in our part of Burgundy, but on wet cold days the muted "thunk" of *contre-grêle* mortars reminded us of the ever-present danger. As I lifted my glass in response to Maire Thévenin's toast to St. Grégoire and looked down the long table, lined with pale-browed, ruddy-faced *vignerons,* I thought whimsically to myself that if—just if—St. Grégoire failed to negotiate a perfect harvest and someone suffered a caprice of nature, Roland would write a petition of complaint, all would sign, and in time reparations would somehow be made. Addended, in contrast to my whimsy, was a thought of Tommy's lonely figure silhouetted against that golden prairie sky shaking his fist at the departing squall that had destroyed his crop.

Once the harvest was begun, the mood of our village, indeed the mood of the whole Côte d'Or, seemed to change. The grapes were good, the fair weather promised to hold. A guarded optimism replaced the previous week's taut suspense. St. Romain was suddenly empty. Only the small grocery store was open for a few hours early in the morning. Every able hand was in the vineyards picking grapes from morning till night. From my studio window I watched the large two-wheeled carts roll noisily back and forth, bringing in the wine. The aroma of fermenting juice filled the nostrils with every breath. It was extremely hard to stay at my drawing board, but there seemed always to be an urgent deadline to meet so I forced myself to paint until at least noon every day. Then Dene and I would roam the countryside. Almost everyone was too busy to stop and talk, but often I would be invited to step inside a cellar for a quick taste of the *vin doux,* the fermenting wine in its early stages, still quite sweet and grapy but filled with bubbles that sizzled pleasantly in the mouth like champagne. Once Dene started to accompany me inside a cellar, but the *vigneron* smilingly blocked her way. "On n'peut pas laisser entrer les dames," he explained. "The fermentation might stop."

The vineyards of the Côte d'Or are for the most part divided into small parcels owned usually by the individuals who farm them. A single vineyard such as, to take a well-

known example, Clos de Vougeot may have many different *propriétaires.* Virtually every *propriétaire-vigneron* is also his own vintner, and picks, crushes, and ferments his own grapes according to his own judgment and preference, then markets his own wine or sells it in bulk to a *négociant,* who blends it with other appropriate *vignerons'* wines. The *négociant,* who is often also an *éleveur,* which means, in this case, something like "manager," will then supervise the development of the wine, barrel-aging some, storing others in large vats, bottling each when he feels, or his market demands, that he should do so. An *éleveur-négociant* might or might not also be a "shipper," who would place the finished wine into the market stream along which it would flow eventually into the consumer's mouth. This multifarious handling is considered by some to be beneficial. The rationale is that many sophisticated judgments are brought to bear on the final product, thereby insuring that it will be of the utmost quality possible. Others disparage it by reasoning that in the course of vinification, blending, and aging, all of which may possibly be carried out by different people, the individual expression of the winemaker as "artist" is lost or at least diminished.

I could not recommend either point of view without hedging. A vineyard region divided among so many different producers without knowledgeable intermediaries would result in a consumer-purchaser's nightmare. The grower-*négociant*-shipper chain, which permits the accumulation of a sufficient volume of wines of comparable origin and quality, *does* permit the sale of wines of very *particular* character, which otherwise could not be generally enjoyed.

On the other hand, the exquisite pleasure of drinking

a wine unique to a small perfectly situated bit of soil in a perfect *climat,* fermented and tenderly finished by a fine winemaker with a sensitivity evolved during a lifetime of personal acquaintance with his materials, is an experience which— Well, my old friend Milton once tried to explain happiness to me, saying, "Ifn you ain't nevah been a black man on Satiday night, with a week's pay in yo pocket . . . mistuh, you jest ain't really been alive!" I have a feeling that the experience of near ecstasy which he was trying to express may well be very close to the experience I would like to convey here.

As the harvest season drew to a close and the wine proved to be good and reasonably plentiful, the traditional warmth and generosity for which Burgundy is justly famous became more and more apparent. Henri Latour and Maire Thévenin introduced me to even more of their friends than I had met earlier. Dene and I renewed our acquaintance with Monsieur Noblé at the Domaine de la Romanée-Conti. We tasted the new wines and our conversations drew out questions of comparison with the older wines; these, in turn, led to speculation about which of the characteristics perceived would endure as well as those of the vintage of '57 or '45— and so on, into many an afternoon. To paraphrase Milton: "If you've never been a well-introduced thirsty American in a well-stocked Burgundian cellar, just after a fine harvest when everyone was feeling relaxed and eager to show off to a fellow winemaker, mon vieux, tu n'en comprend point vivre!"

To return to the question of marketing Burgundy's cornucopia of wines, I think I would have to support the *négociant* system as being a very practical method. But the experience of being able to taste hundreds of wines at their source of origin, poured or pipetted by their growers before they were sold to *négociants,* left me haunted by the wish that my inspiring experience could be shared with others, and it was to shape the part of my own winemaking career that still lay ahead.

The months and years in Burgundy that followed our first one were a pleasant mixture of experiences and impressions. I was constantly impressed with the insistence upon, and seriousness of, special events in the life of the whole region, all connected to the production and enjoyment of wine. I have mentioned the Fête de St. Vincent but there were others. In addition, the spirit of camaraderie and friendship were everywhere, always shared with good wine and wonderful food.

The after-harvest glow of good spirits seemed to increase as the leaves fell and the *enjambeur* tractors hilled up the vines for winter. The bars of the local "country" restaurants, which were often much like old-fashioned American boardinghouse tables, where extra places were set when guests came in, were filled with red-cheeked *vignerons* animatedly swapping stories. Our first-course fare for luncheon shifted from the *écrevisses,* or crawfish, so plentiful in the summer, which we had washed down with ample amounts of young local *blancs,* most often made by the restaurateur, to snails. This, however, was a personal whim rather than a seasonal dictate. Snails are consumed locally, probably in greater quantities, during the leafy season of the grapevines, from which the snails draw their sustenance. I have seen grape pickers build small fires in the vineyards at mealtime breaks to roast fresh-caught *escargots,* picking out the hot

rubbery meats, dipping them into a prepared sauce of garlic, parsley, and butter. In the evenings we ate whatever was being served, and this country fare was extremely good. *Coq au vin, boeuf marchand du vin, poulet femme-de-bourgogne,* fish of all sorts, game, terrines of country pâtés, mushrooms, fruit, truffles. I fell in love with *sanglier,* the meat of the local wild pigs, dangerous to hunt because of their aggressive disposition, the boars armed with short vicious tusks. The wines were either *rouge* or *blanc,* often with no label, drawn by the *propriétaire* from the barrels in his own cellar each morning, sometimes stoppered with a cork, more often with a small plastic snap-on. They were usually young. They were always good.

In some of the local places, such as the nearby Hôtel des Roches in St. Romain, we sometimes met with Monsieur Thévenin, his mother, Madame Buonaterra, or some member of his staff for lunch or apéritif. This gave us a kind of comfortable credibility with local people we might otherwise not have been able to establish. They loved to joke with me, tell me the legendary tall tales of Burgundian mythology. There is a touch of Tartarin in every Frenchman, a *petit soupçon* of Paul Bunyan in every American. We pulled each other's legs joyfully. Roland himself set the pace. Large banners, posted throughout his offices and cellars, declared, "Sans St. Romain, l'amour est vain!"

"I thought it was the wines of Provence which were the best aphrodisiac," I challenged.

"Bah! C'était le Duke Robert lui-même qui buvait un flagon de St. Romain chaque soir et sa fécondité était légendaire!"

"Qui boit du bourgogne vivait toujours" was another favorite boast.

"My father is eighty-five," I teased, "never touched anything stronger than water. His father before him lived to be ninety-nine," I exaggerated a little, "both teetotalers."

"Shh," loudly in mock concern, from a red-cheeked elderly man standing nearby. "Doucement! On doit pas répéter un tel bruit en public, je vous en prie. Écoutez, monsieur. There used to be an old ivrogne who lived near here. Artiste, comme vous. He attended a funeral service in the neighboring village of Bouzie, conducted by a young priest from Paris who was new in the region and who did not approve of drinking. He praised the deceased for his long life of temperance and splendid health. He had, the priest emphasized, lived to be one hundred and three years old without ever touching a drop of alcohol of any kind, even wine. The old artist was devoted to the wines of St. Romain and consumed at least a bottle with every meal, sometimes two. The sermon troubled him deeply. He had noticed a bit of discomfort lately, 'avec son foie.' That evening after mass he approached the young priest. 'Cette longévité,' he asked, referring to the deceased centenarian, 'was it unique in his family?' The young priest reluctantly admitted that he didn't personally know any other members of the family, but after some hesitation, he added that there did seem to be an older brother who was still alive at the age of one hundred and five. He had not been seen sober for the past sixty years and had not been able to attend the services." The red-cheeked raconteur tapped my chest with a pointed forefinger. "Examine votre family tree again, monsieur," he said gravely. "You must to find a skeleton in the closet."

In mid-November, there is a magnificent three-day celebration in the Côte d'Or known appropriately as "Les Trois Glorieuses," whose purpose is to provide an environment of festivity in which the central event, the auction of the wines belonging to the Hôtel-Dieu at the Hospice de Beaune on the morning of the second day, will be properly dramatized. These wines are produced by more than one hundred acres of magnificent vineyards, which have been given to the Hôtel-Dieu, the hospital of Beaune, over the centuries by grateful Burgundians. Their sale produces income for the betterment of medical services and facilities in the splendid institution, which was founded by Chancellor Nicolas Rolin in 1443 and is still housed in the beautiful and perfectly preserved medieval building in which it originated. The sale also has another important function in that the prices brought by the various wines are considered to be an important indicator of the quality of the year's vintage and strongly affect the price of the rest of the Côte d'Or's wines for that year.

On the first day the wines to be auctioned the next afternoon are available for tasting in the cellars of the hospices, and a long line forms early to purchase tickets to enter. Inside the vast arched and vaulted cellar, barrel after barrel of the young wines about to be put on the block are attended by *vignerons* standing by with *voleurs*, or pipettes, to draw the wine from the barrels. Many of the wines are still yeasty and *pétillant*, filling the cool cellar air with a heady perfume. It takes a few moments for the eyes to get adjusted to the dim candlelit cellars and to realize that the place is crowded with buyers from all over the world, *tastevins* in hand, carefully tasting and talking about the wines. On the evening of the first day there is a dinner with the Confrérie des Chevaliers du Tastevin at the Clos de Vougeot, the men all dressed in dark suits, the women looking elegant in formal gowns, coiffed with the special chic that seems to be second nature to the French.

Trumpets announce the events of the evening and festivities as they unfold. One is the ceremony of *intronisation*, in which new members are struck lightly on each shoulder, as if being knighted, by the trunk of a grapevine instead of a sword; then the red-and-golden-ribboned *tastevin*, symbol of membership in the Confrérie, is placed around the neck, and short speeches are delivered, all in high good humor, usually archly spoofing. Food service and the pouring of the wines accompanying each course are preceded, for example, by a sudden fusillade of shotguns, which immediately hushes all conversation and focuses all eyes on costumed trumpeters, whose coiled horns announce a parade of paired hunters, carrying between them freshly shot pheasant suspended from a rod. Later a file of young *sous-chefs* supporting enormous platters of whole roasted pigs will appear, drawing applause from the wine-warmed diners. The Cadets de Bourgogne, dressed in the black aprons of *cavists,* wittily intersperse the traditional drinking songs of Burgundy. "Le vin est très bon pour les femmes," one of them puckishly observes between songs, "quand il est buvez par les hommes."

The spirit of conviviality is periodically reinforced by someone calling for a *ban bourgignon,* whereupon all guests lift their arms to a simple little chanted ditty, accompanied by clapping hands, which momentarily diverts everyone's attention and insures that no conversation can go on too long. The dinner can last six hours, yet it seems only a few charmed moments, as though one has been transported back in time to one of the fabled feasts of the old dukes of Burgundy.

The second day the wine auction is held. Each lot of wine is presented for bidding during the burning of three small candles, the highest bid before the expiration of the last candle being the *gagneur.* It is a beautiful scene. The judges or monitors of the auction are all in black and are seated in a long row behind a scarlet-draped table on an elevated stage running the full width of the large room. Behind them hang enormous medieval tapestries belonging

to the priceless collection of the Hôtel-Dieu's museum. Below the stage, silhouetted against the red drapery, sits the auction's secretary at a small desk. A crowd of perhaps a thousand people fill the hall, and through its glassed walls perhaps a thousand more watch from the street outside. A low tense buzz of hushed conversation rises and falls as the bidding proceeds. The dark-suited monitors jab pointed fingers toward the bidders to identify them. A spattering of congratulatory applause sporadically breaks out in one or another part of the hall as the wine of a great vineyard is bid on frantically to the very last sputter of the third candle.

If prices are good, a general air of contentment prevails after the auction. Newspapers all over France will carry the news as headlines. The next morning the Beaune and other local newspapers will have pages of photos of the event. All wines will get a better price because of the favorable publicity.

That night there is a celebratory dinner, the Dîner aux Chandelles, in the cavernous cellars of the Hôtel-Dieu. In contrast to the rollicking joviality of the Cadets at the Clos de Vougeot the previous evening, the musical fare this evening is sweetly mellow, equally transporting to another time frame, medieval still, but in yet another mood, *gracieuse, plein de luxe.*

The third of the "three glorious days" presents another, totally different aspect of Burgundian life and tradition. This is the Paulée, the day of the *vigneron,* the men and women of the soil, those blunt-fingered, pale-browed *trogne-rouge* toilers-in-the-vineyard, whose sturdy bodies and unquenchable good spirits provide the enormous physical effort without which nature and the earth would not so bountifully yield the glorious blessings of this fabled land. The character and innate symbolism of this day resemble somewhat that of our Thanksgiving.

The core of the day's celebration is a gargantuan feast in a local restaurant at noon. Each guest brings his own wine to this event, symbolizing the earlier origins of the Paulée, when it was no doubt a totally communal gathering of neighboring *vignerons,* the *patrons* and their *ouvriers* celebrating the end of the *vendange.* Soon there is a forest of bottles along the tables and then there is the sound of popping corks as the diners open and pour their own wines. Bottles are passed along the table as the winegrowers try each other's wines.

Course after course of food is served by young women dressed in traditional bonnets and embroidered blouses, peasant costumes that are, except for being crisp and clean, remarkably like the garb worn weeks earlier in the vineyards during harvest. Informal, casual conviviality in the manner of a church supper is the style of the afternoon, with guests moving about from table to table, chatting about their daily affairs. Occasionally there is a speech. More often there is a song. *Bans bourgignons* break out impishly, as spontaneous as laughter, which fills the ear constantly. The one serious event of the afternoon is a traditional award of one hundred bottles of Meursault wine for a major work of excellence in the field of literature.

There are many versions of the apocryphal legend of St. Vincent, whose day is celebrated in January, each year in a different Burgundian town. One that had considerable currency in Burgundy goes something like this: It was noticed by the heavenly powers that the people of Burgundy, though properly respectful and attendant to their religious duties, appeared to be very content under their heavy burden of mortal toil, and even though they labored long and arduously from dawn till dark there was no note of discontent in their prayers, no anguished plea for relief in their dutifully upturned eyes. They were happy. And also they lived uncommonly long and healthy lives. Young St. Vincent was delegated to descend to earth and investigate the reason for such contentment. Weeks went by with no report. At last a second delegate was sent to investigate, and Vincent was found to have indeed discovered the immediate earthly blessings for which Burgundians so willingly postponed the promised beneficences of heaven. He was filled with them. In fact he was overwhelmed by them—quite drunk in a Burgundian cellar "ses pieds contre la mur—sa tête au-dessous un robinet." After deliberate consideration his name was removed from the rolls of heavenly saints—but the winegrowers of Burgundy, and incidentally of virtually every other part of France as well, adopted him as their very own patron saint, and so his anniversary day is celebrated every year.

When it fell to St. Romain to host the Fête de St. Vincent, *vigneron* societies from more than fifty wine villages of the Côte d'Or gathered in our tiny hamlet to form a cortège, led by local schoolchildren dressed in the ancient costumes of the region. Silver *tastevins* around their necks, each society displayed its statue of St. Vincent on a litter carried by two *vignerons.* Marches were played by several bands but the marchers paid little heed to the cadence. The climax, of course, was another magnificent luncheon, graced as always by magnificent wines.

This lunch was to be more than usually memorable for me as I was seated with the famous Chanoine Kir, whose legendary importance in the region of Burgundy rivaled that of St. Vincent. I had met the chanoine before and he kindly remembered this, greeting me warmly as we sat down to dine. Two waiters with apparently no other duties than the assurance of Monsieur Kir's convenience and pleasure

flanked our position. From his seventy-five years of service to Burgundy, as one of its most honored citizens and a hero of the war, he was reputed to know every cellar of Burgundy and just what the choicest wines were, wherever he went. He kept his two *garçons* scurrying, whispering inquiringly in their ears about a certain vintage or another and then liberally pouring the wine they brought into every glass within his reach. It was extremely hard to stay sober in his presence. Consequently, I remember very few details of our conversation but, rather, retain a vivid impression of the remarkable old man's heroic capacity for wine and the memory of an extraordinary euphoria sustained by the chorus known as Les Joyeux Bourguignons, singing *chansons à boire.* Somehow, every time I look at the little stone statue of St. Vincent that now stands in the entryway of Benmarl, I see the face of Monsieur Kir.*

There were two important events that occurred while we lived in France which played a part in our eventual return to Marlboro. One was the sale of a piece of land that adjoined the upper vineyards of Benmarl, which I read about in a copy of the local paper that had been forwarded. This was property I had hoped to buy myself because it provided not only additional planting space but would give our whole property, especially the site most desirable for a new home, access to a good town road. Without this land the only way to reach the site I had in mind was limited to the very narrow machinery road up the east face of the hill, which was too steep to permit year-round passage of most cars. This prevented the building of a residence or other use of that part of the farm and also, of course, limited its market value. I

*The old chanoine died two years later, and his passing was mourned in virtually all major European publications. *Life International* carried a multipaged pictorial history of his life, as seventy-five-year *maire* of Dijon, *doyen* of Burgundy and a hero of the war years. In his honor Paris bars and restaurants began immediately to serve his favorite drink, a little white wine of Burgundy with a splash of cassis. "Un kir, s'il vous plait" caught on overnight in Europe, and today the mention of the word "kir" will produce that drink anywhere in the world.

wrote a letter immediately to the land's new owner, offering to buy an access strip from the town road to my vineyards at a price liberally higher than the current land value. In less than two weeks he accepted my proposal and I completed the purchase by mail. For the first time in the busy years since we had moved abroad I let myself dream of returning to Benmarl to live, but it was to be more than two years before our family affairs would finally arrange themselves for our return.

The second event was hearing from the farmer who was filling in for me at Benmarl, giving notice of his decision to leave and move on. In my search for a replacement to manage the farm I even advertised in the Beaune newspaper, but none of the young men who responded seemed quite right. To my surprise my friend Henri Latour expressed some interest in moving to America, though there were strong family ties that made this unlikely. Of course Benmarl would have to be converted from a hobby to a business adequate to support him and make a reasonable profit for me. I suggested we visit Benmarl together at my expense to help him make up his mind. The upshot was a memorable trip, during which Henri got his first taste of the United States and I got the benefit of his assessment and advice concerning my vineyard and its future prospects.

When Henri and I walked up the hill at Benmarl to inspect the upper vineyards, it was obvious they were not in good condition. Underpruned and underfertilized, they were very low in vigor. I could see Henri was not impressed with the attention they had been getting, so I tried to turn our conversation to my plans for the future. We would reshape the eastern face of the hill, terracing it into shelves wide enough to carry tractors and harvesting vehicles. It was obvious, though, that the newly developed mechanical harvesters he had admired couldn't operate on such a hill as ours. He carried a little pad and made notes as we walked over the land, calculating the cost of putting the entire property into production. For him this project had to make realistic financial sense if he was going to give up his land rights to his family's vineyard.

The next day we measured the barn and figured the costs of converting it into a working winery sufficiently large to be practical. As I gradually saw the whole project of vineyard repair and replanting and winery construction take shape in his mind, I could also see that he was going to finally arrive at a much higher overall cost than I had ever envisioned.

"Environ d'un million," Henri said hesitantly a few days later when, back in his home in Auxey-Duresses, I pressed him for an estimate of the costs. "Whew," I exhaled softly. "Je parle en francs françaises naturellement," he added, seeing my expression. Still, $200,000 was even more than I had expected—certainly more than I could afford. He could be off a bit, of course, but only on building items. Virtually all of our equipment would have to come from Europe, and he was perfectly familiar with costs there. "Désolé," he said sympathetically.

I was unable, any longer, to make myself believe that I could expect a foreigner to take over my farm successfully and permit me to continue working abroad.

Soon Henri was caught up completely in the life he had always lived and the *fantaisie* of America faded. I arranged my painting schedule to permit me to go back again to New York and persuade a local farmer to pick my grapes and sell them to home winemakers at his fruit stand. It was awkward, to say the least, to be continually flying back and forth to tend to the farm, but for the present there was no other solution. I could not afford to give up my art business in Europe and become a gentleman farmer in Marlboro, nor could I afford to convert the farm into even a modest business. This would have to wait until the boys were college age and we could all go home. In the meantime I could only occasionally visit Benmarl's magnificent hill, where I would build my wine château, and dream of the changes and improvements I would make in the winery.

chapter VII

Return to America

When our attention was finally refocused on Benmarl in
1967 I realized that my experiences in Burgundy had solid-
ified my early fancies regarding its potential future. The
whim that had led me so blithely to buy the old vineyard
as a pastime had now become a vision of my farm as a kind
of model for a cottage industry of small premium-quality
wine producers. Mr. Wardell's disillusioned reference to the
apple-tree-filled valley as a place "growing babyfood" had
become in my mind the "Côte d'Or" of America. But, as I
became reacquainted with my country, I realized as I had
never done before what a difficult, perhaps impossible, task
was ahead for us. The state of viniculture in eastern America
was at its lowest historical ebb. The large established New
York wineries were still making the sweet grapy confections
which had never found, and could never find, a place on
serious wine drinkers' tables, and, worse, they had given all
New York wines a poor and deteriorating reputation.

Even though the population of the United States in
general was showing considerable interest in good dry wines
for use at the table, no truly understanding efforts had been
made in the East, on a major scale, to produce such wines,
much less the indigenous, regional table wines in the Euro-

pean style which I felt were possible, and indeed *must* be
made if there was to be an eastern wine industry. In fact, the
management of these companies seemed bewilderingly determined to prevent the development of regional, indigenous wines. As their percentage of the wine sales in the
American market dropped every year, by reason of the
steady increase in the consumption of California wine, New
York and other eastern wineries bought large volumes of the
cheapest bulk California wine and shipped it across the
country in enormous tank cars to blend with their own
fermentations. The result was compounded disaster. By
adding the poorest-quality, desert-grown western vinifera
to the "foxiest" eastern labrusca varieties, they made wines
that were far worse than any of the components could possibly have made alone. Consequently, eastern wine's share of
a growing market was dropping lower and lower and so was
its reputation.

We were incredulous. As we looked at the situation
from the perspective of our experience, the failure of the
management of the eastern wine industry to understand
what was happening appeared incomprehensibly naïve, and
in view of the fact that its blindness was leading a major part
of New York's agricultural industry into a dead-end street,
it seemed only marginally short of criminal.

We knew from our own private experimental work, and
of course from Philip Wagner's and Everett Crosby's, that
eastern vineyards were capable of producing good wine
grapes, and we knew from the experience of sharing our
own wines with sophisticated European connoisseurs that
eastern wines, properly made, *could* compare favorably with
many of the world's best. Why was no one rushing to create
new vineyards to supply this important growing market?

Actually there *were* a small number of very talented
winemakers working in the East by this time, and there *were*
also a few far-sighted people in the management of the
established wineries. Dr. Konstantin Frank, the strong-
willed, colorful Russian immigrant who understood that the

eastern climate could support European wine-grape varieties, had been recognized by Charles Fornier, president of the Gold Seal Wine Company, and employed by him to carry out experimental work in their vineyards. During our absence numerous other professional and amateur grape growers had read and been persuaded by Philip Wagner's books to grow grapes and make wine. There was a kind of ground swell of interest in wine in the entire United States, which included amateur and professional winemakers as well as casual consumers. America's affluent citizenry were traveling back to the countries of origin of its polyglot population and finding that somehow, in the creation of this wonderful materially rich new world, a number of worthwhile aesthetic virtues of the old world had been left behind —among them the enjoyment of wine as a part of one's everyday meals.

A virtual revolution in the eating and drinking habits of our nation was quietly taking place. However, it seemed to us that neither the scope nor the nature of this revolution was clearly understood—even in California, where the first source for fine European-style American wine was just beginning to appear. Recognition of the significance of the entrepreneurial "boutique" wineries, which eventually wrested the leadership from California's winemaking establishment, had not yet occurred. I remember a piece in *Wines and Vines,* the industry magazine (not then owned by Philip Hiaring), rather patronizingly congratulating James D. Zellerbach on his tiny, beautifully equipped winery. The opinion of the writer was that it was a "nice toy" but of course, with such emphasis on individualism and given its small scale of operations, it could never make it in the real world. The writer of the piece was not usually short-sighted. The realization that a significant portion of the American public could *recognize* the subtleties inherent in fine individually made wines and would *pay* to obtain them just had not penetrated the minds of the California industry leadership. This blindness was even more typical of the eastern industry.

As disappointing as these realizations were, there was very little time for our thoughts to dwell on them. I had come back full of inspiration instilled by Burgundy, confident as I reassessed my vineyards and even my simple little winery that all the essentials for making good wine were here. Somehow I had made reasonably decent wines here before. Their acceptance in France had given credence to that. Now I must settle down to learning how to repeat these successes at will, encourage others to do the same, and try to find ways to persuade the American public to drink them.

First I must put what I had learned into practice. Taking a cue from Henri Latour's experiment with tall vine trellises (which he had been inspired to try by the writings of Dr. Nelson Shaulis of the New York Agricultural Experiment Station), I began to retrain all of my own vines. This was a rather long and tedious process, stretching over many months. When Dene returned we patiently strung an additional higher wire on each row of vines, this one at about my eye level, then bent a pair of one-year-old canes upward and tied them in opposite directions along the new top wire. As the buds along these higher canes pushed out shoots, the developing curtain of leaves presented a greatly increased surface to absorb the sun's rays. In order to increase further the proportion of leaf surface to the number of grapes to be ripened, we also began the practice of removing one of the three to four incipient grape clusters which each young shoot produces as it makes its early spring growth. Thus all the energy the shoot would have previously expended to ripen three or four clusters could now be concentrated on ripening only two clusters. This resulted, we found, in much more mature fruit in a shorter growing period and, surprisingly, in a very small reduction in total juice production. This technique of vineyard management was also being recommended by New York's Dr. Shaulis, but I learned it secondhand from Henri in Burgundy.

Also I began to make small changes in my winemaking practices. Beginning with the very first harvest after returning, we stored our red wines in the oak barrels we had brought back with us from St. Romain. Although we had previously employed oak barrels for wine storage, they had been used, charred whiskey barrels, which had always imparted a hint of bourbon taste and aroma to the wines. The difference in the effect of storage in the new Nevers oak was immediately and agreeably discernible. Previously I had never been willing to wait later than January or February before bottling my small production of wine. Now I determined to wait until late spring at least in order to allow the absorption of more of the tannins from the fresh barrels, which gave the wine a pleasant astringency and more complex flavor, with vanilla-like overtones, than I had ever obtained before. As the weather warmed and the temperature in the well-insulated barn cellar rose slightly, I noticed that the wine stored in the French barrels became gassy, and I realized that it was experiencing the malo-lactic fermentation that Burgundian winemakers consider to be essential. Since I had never been able to induce this phenomena before, I concluded that the bacteria which caused it had somehow been transported in the new barrels from the storage cellar of the *tonnelier* in St. Romain. This fortunate occurrence was repeated spontaneously each subsequent year that these barrels were kept in use.

When the wine became tranquil I bottled it. Again I resisted the temptation to drink it all directly as I had done in the past, forcing myself to lay away about three hundred bottles, or the equivalent of one barrel, of the red wines. In every way that I could I imitated the practices I had seen used in Burgundy. I couldn't say with certainty even to this day that this meticulous imitation was the reason for the change in character of the wines I made that first year and most of those that followed. A number of other favorable factors undoubtedly contributed. My vines were now much more mature. I had been away for a number of years. The Baco and Foch vineyards, which were the source of the red wines being made in the French barrels, were now nearly nine years old, a fact which in Europe is associated with improved wine quality. Also we had a series of very dry, hot summers producing small but very sweet grapes. Perhaps as important as any other factor was that my expectations as to what my new wine should taste like were totally different than ever before. Previous to my intimate association with Burgundian wine at its source I had never tasted a young Burgundy wine directly from the barrel or, in fact, even tasted one in bottle younger than four or five years. I had judged my own freshly made wines against mature La Tâche or Grands-Éschézaux, found them lacking, and guzzled them in bemused but merry despair.

Now, with the memory of baby Burgundies in my mouth, I began to find similarities, which gave me hope that I was on the right track. Also I began to develop the patience to put off my judgment until I had valid comparisons to make between my wines and others in the same stage of development. I realized that my technological understanding of wine was not great, so I read voraciously everything I could find to improve it. Gradually over the next few vintages I became more confident that my results were actual improvements.

Meantime, the growth of amateur winemaking in America seemed explosive. We could have easily sold all our grapes to home winemakers. Interest in wine was rampant.

Dene and I were participants at the founding meeting of The American Wine Society. The organization of this group was a very significant phenomenon in the early development of the eastern wine revolution. Although the initiative was provided by amateur winemakers, virtually all of the first entrepreneurs of the approaching eastern wine revolution were present. Dr. Konstantin Frank was host for the meeting. His winery was already licensed and doing business as "Vinifera Wine Cellars." Also there were Dr. Hamilton Mowbray, whose plantings for his Montbray winery in Maryland were approaching production; Douglas Moorhead, of Presque Isle vineyards; Al Wiederkehr, who was planning to change the direction of his four-generation family winery in Altus, Arkansas; Walter Taylor, who was shortly to begin his famous feud with *his* family's well-known wine company and set up his Bully Hill winery; and many others.

Unfortunately the potential effectiveness of the incipient professionals in this group was to be severely hampered by the polarization of opinion into a diversionary controversy over which grapevines were the best. The most strident group, centered around Dr. Frank, adamantly insisted that only the old classic European vinifera varieties already identified with the world's most highly respected wines should be planted at all. Others more cautiously felt that, although these vines did indeed make superb wines in very special microclimates and particular soils, the very same grapes equally often made indifferent-to-frankly-bad wines in other environments. These winemakers, who identified with Philip Wagner, took the position that certain new crossbred or hybrid varieties seemed better suited to eastern climates and soils and in fact when grown in appropriate environments were capable of equal or better quality than the vinifera.

It seemed that more invective was being generated than good wine, and this tempest-over-a-glass-of-wine was hampering what should have been a cooperative learning process. Both groups of antagonists were, of course, partly right and made some excellent wines to prove it.

Dene, the boys, and I tried to keep a foot in both camps. We certainly liked the vinifera wines, which were most often at the center of the controversy: Chardonnay and Riesling among the whites, Pinot Noir and Cabernet Sauvignon among the reds. We knew them quite intimately in many of their manifestations around the world, but it was extremely hard to support the concept that they were automatically going to insure high quality wherever they were planted, when we had tasted so many examples which were not very good. Also my current experiences making wine from hybrid grapes employing the techniques usually reserved in Europe for only the vinifera seemed to me to be resulting in wines of astonishing quality—different, but as good as most vinifera I had ever tasted. The point we had the most difficulty with among the vinifera-only camp was their insistence that *only* their grapes made the best wines. Well, best in what frame of reference? If wine was to be regarded as a food, which we felt to be appropriate, and it was to be judged in a context where its contribution to a specific culinary combination was to be the frame, then *no* wine would be universally best. As a painter I couldn't help but feel that the restriction imposed by the vinifera-only group was comparable to insisting that there were only certain "good" colors, or perhaps a better analogy would be that there is only one "good" painting style. Such oversimplification in the name of purism seemed more amateurish than sophisticated to us, and more often than not we found it to be espoused by those with narrow backgrounds or short wine-drinking experience.

It seemed then and still seems to me most unlikely that the grapes that will be in use fifty years or less from now will be the same as those being used for winemaking today. As demand increases for wines from the world's most famous small regions, their vineyards are being forced to expand into less favorable soil and climate conditions, and efforts are already now being made in many regions to modify their grapes genetically so they may better adapt to the new conditions. Soon all wine grapes may well be hybrids and wine will probably be the better for it, just as corn is better today and various other fruits, legumes, and cereals are better for having been crossbred to bring out their better qualities in different growing environments. The essential question was not which was the best grape but simply which combinations of grape varieties, soils, climate—and winemakers— were capable of producing good-tasting wines that could be useful in complementing our evolving American cuisine. This would take a great deal of time and work to determine.

Not all of the work to be done would require great knowledge or training, just patience and time. Our own years of experimenting at Benmarl, when we had borrowed what we could from Crosby in New York, Wagner in Maryland, and Galet in France, had to be matched by similar work by many others. Dozens of wine-minded grape growers had to plant dozens of the thought-to-be-good wine varieties in order to see which performed best in the various soils and microclimates of various regions, to try dozens of ways of vineyard management, to prune long or short, to fertilize or not (and how much?), to cluster-thin or not (if so, how much?), to control the ratio of leaf surface to fruit production (to what degree?). . . . The list of hypotheses to be proposed and tested was limited only by the imagination.

In addition to such vineyard research, winemakers with a reasonable understanding of laboratory technique and a *considerable* understanding of good wine, which could only be gained by drinking experience, had to carry out even more experimentation—endless combinations of grape varieties in different stages of ripeness, fermented warm or cold (how cold?), in stainless steel or wooden barrels, under hundreds of varying conditions. Then would come the waiting. . . . Some wines are only good when young, others develop interesting character when older (how much older?). Only time and trial could provide the understanding needed. To further complicate the matter, few of the answers to be sought were really amenable to any absolute judgment. Winemaking is first an art, and maxims such as "beauty is in the eye of the beholder" or "taste is a relative matter" warn all artists and all winemakers that the result of their work is not likely to be a formula—only another point of view.

In view of this need for extensive, widespread empirical experimentation, I thought wistfully of our efforts years earlier to make it possible for individual farmers to produce and sell wine as their end product as so many Europeans did. If we had succeeded then with our idea of creating "farm wineries," perhaps there would by now be an accumulation of common regional winemaking experience upon which the much-needed empirical experimentation program could be based.

We tried to persuade some of our local apple farmers to put in a few acres of wine grapes but they answered my persuasions with a question, "Who would buy them?" In our immediate area farmers had experienced a number of very bad years one after another, and in the little farm villages some of the best fruit land was being sold off to unrestricted developers. Efforts to stop the breaking up of large farming parcels by creating zoning regulations forbidding building on small lots in agricultural areas were defeated by the farmers themselves. Why should they be forced to become the stewards of the community's reserve of farm land, paying ever-rising taxes in an economy returning them ever-dropping profits? The youngsters of some fine old farm families were discouraged by the bleak prospects they saw for farming, and they were taking jobs in town or moving away. This was a bad situation, for when the young leave, farms die. A compelling sense of urgency spurred us to increase our efforts to encourage the planting of wine grapes. I volunteered to speak at farm meetings. With the help of the local Extension Service and the professors from the New York Experiment Station at Geneva, New York, as much emphasis as possible was given the idea that wine drinking was becoming a part of our national eating habits and there should soon be an excellent market for suitable grapes. No response.

Finally we came to realize that the idea was just too new. There was not yet enough evidence of demand for wine grapes to persuade our practical fellow farmers to make the investment required to establish new vineyards. *We* would have to set the example ourselves and create a demand. After all, *we* were the believers. We had small but already established vineyards, and by this time we had acquired almost twenty-five years of thoughtful winemaking

and wine-drinking experience, a good part of it in the vineyards and in the company of some of the world's greatest
winemakers.

Actually, of course, this was very much what I wanted
to do, but my early experiences had made me wary and
Roland Thévenin's warning kept rising in my memory:
"C'est okay comme violon, but, mon cher ami, can you
afford eet?"

Could sufficient funds come from the end of an artist's
brush? I was afraid not. Certainly not the amount estimated
by Henri Latour to expand our operations sufficiently to
support two families. Even now, it seemed that every time
I got up from the drawing board the tractor ran out of gas.

The truth was that we would prefer that our little project *not* become a business in the usual sense of the word. I
had a profession as an artist that I enjoyed. Dene was now
looking forward to a new professional career of her own as
a psychologist. We really wanted our farm to remain a sort
of private research station—to provide assistance to a renaissance of winegrowing in our region and help keep our valley
green and rural; to serve as a model *for,* rather than to *be,* a
winery business—to have our cake and eat it too.

We decided to build on top of the hill a studio for me
that could also be, in part, a small practical winery. I had
been planning it since the purchase of the access strip to
Highland Avenue, doodling little sketches on the margins of
my paintings for the last couple of years. A pair of large
bronze door handles I had designed in Paris and cast in
London for its entry were waiting to have doors built for
them.

Since there was no town water supply, it was necessary
to drill a well. I called Fred Robinson, vice-president of the
local bank, an ebulliently friendly, helpful man who
managed to know everyone and everything that went on in
our village. "Call Jimmy Eckerson. Best well driller in the
valley," he said.

"I want a really good well," I cautioned, thinking of the

possible future needs of the winery and remembering the problems we had had with a well we had drilled for the lower part of the farm. It had yielded barely two and a half gallons of flow per minute, even at a depth of five hundred feet, and often ran dry while filling a spray tank. "Jimmy's your man," Fred insisted. I was reassured when the drilling rig arrived. The equipment was modern, well kept. Jimmy was obviously competent. "Where do you want to dig?" he asked.

"You tell me," I countered. "The studio-winery will sit there," I said, pointing to the north side of a clearing I had made. "The barn will face it on the opposite side."

By then Dene had made preliminary drawings for a residence to occupy the east side of the court, but early bids two or three times higher than she expected had shown us we were not in touch with the realities of the inflating American economy.

"There might be a residence there," I said, pointing.

"Hmm," Jim replied, pulling out of his pocket an odd-looking Y-shaped brass gadget. "So right about there would be pretty good, wouldn't it?"

"Perfect," I agreed.

He grasped the gadget, holding it in the manner of a diviner's branch and began to walk solemnly back and forth across the clearing. Almost precisely in the center of the clearing, exactly where it obviously would be most convenient, the point of the brass fork plunged downward. "We'll dig here," he said.

I telephoned Fred. "I thought divining rods went out with witchcraft."

"What've you got against witchcraft?" Fred said. "Trust Jimmy."

I looked around uneasily as the drilling rig was set up. The land around us fell away sharply in all directions. We were drilling on the very highest point of the farm. If I had only been able to get two gallons a minute at the farmhouse three hundred feet below us at a well depth of five hundred feet, what could I expect here? "Let's see now. If we had to drill down to that other water table at six dollars a foot, plus casing, plumbing, and pump costs—good grief! there wouldn't be any money left for building."

The first thirty-foot drill pipe screwed itself into the ground in a half hour through pure flaky bits of marl. The second unit was attached and in five feet struck the first hint of rock; still the bit dropped smoothly through the black shale. The third extension went into place at sixty feet. The rock was getting hard. Drilling slowed down. "How deep could you go if you had to?" I asked.

"Don't worry, we'll get you water," and almost before the words were out of his mouth, water gushed over the sides of the drill pipe. When we checked the rate of flow we had well over fifteen gallons per minute at just under a hundred feet of depth. Thumbs up! That would handle any needs we might have. I asked to see Jim's gadget. Homemade, it was simply two quarter-inch brass rods attached to a small block. "This is what located the water?" I asked.

"You saw it," he answered.

"Does it ever fail?"

"Well, it didn't this time, did it?" He chuckled. "I'll be back tomorrow with your pump."

The studio-winery building was a simple 25-by-50-foot rectangular structure, but Dene's clever planning made it serve its two functions very well. There were two ground levels. The lower one opened from a rear courtyard through two 8-foot doors on the north side to a tractor garage and shop area, as well as a 25-by-30-foot barrel-storage cellar. The upper level of the building, facing south, was entered through a pair of doors designed to hold my sculptured handles. A small foyer opened on the left to an 18-by-25-foot concrete-floored processing area, into which grapes could be unloaded through an 8-foot door on its west side. This room was designed to hold comfortably Philip Wagner's cast-off 3-ton-per-hour crusher-stemmer, a small motorized basket press, and about 800 gallons of open red fermentation vats. There was space for about 2,000 gallons of white closed-fermentation tanks and perhaps a dozen 50-gallon barrels. A stairway led from this room to the cellar-barrel storage below, which was large enough to hold about 2,500 gallons of combined wooden tanks and barrel storage. There was space for storage of approximately 1,000 bottles under the stairway. A fold-down stairway led from the processing room up to an attic covering the rest of the building; the attic could hold perhaps 500 empty bottle cases. Behind the foyer adjoining processing was a 10-by-11-foot space divided into a small shower-toilet and a combination kitchen-laboratory.

To the right of the entrance foyer was my studio. For someone who had spent much of a thirty-five-year painting career working in cubbyhole, spare-bedroom studios and hotel rooms scattered over western Europe, or hurriedly dabbing on last-minute changes in an art director's office, it was sheer heaven. My drawing board sat next to a pair of glass doors opening north onto a small balcony, from which the vineyards and the entire valley spread in unobstructed glory.

We bought some additional equipment—an eight-hec-toliter Vaslin press from France, some more French barrels, a six-spout siphon bottle-filler—and when we finished we had created an excellent set-up for our dual purposes as we then saw them: a studio in which I could earn the family living and a model winery in which we could carry on our experimental research and which, if it should have to, could produce a little over two thousand gallons of wine a year and store something near two thousand more. Of course we did not then plan to make more than the two hundred gallons permitted under a householder's permit, even though such constraint was frustrating because there was so much more research that needed to be done than this small amount would permit. It forced us to ferment mostly in small lots in five-gallon carboys, as we had always done in the past. Now we were much more interested in working with the techniques we had become familiar with in Burgundy, which could hardly be applied to less than barrel-sized lots. Nonetheless, we carried on the best we could, making some barrel-sized *cuvées* each year with different varieties or blends of grapes and dividing up the remaining permitted volume into carboy-sized units.

In the spring, shortly after the studio-winery was completed, an opportunity came along to sell the part of the farm containing our residence and the cottage we still called Milton's house, as well as the barn, which had been the first winery. The five-acre piece lay along the east side of the major highway that bisected the farm; because of its long road frontage this land had become quite valuable. Its sale would provide enough money to build the residence Dene had planned across the courtyard from the studio. The drawings for the house were already done. We had recently found an excellent builder, who felt he could work within our budget, so we leapt at the chance and closed the deal within a few days.

Before the summer was over the structure was com-

pleted. Like the studio's, its eastern side was almost completely glass, each large window framing a different picture of graceful rolling hills, the Hudson River, and the miles of handsome valley floor, covered with fruit trees and vines, which had enchanted me the first time I had seen it. Although Stan HasBrouck, the builder, had surprised us all by completing his work at a cost within his estimate, every member of the family decided to take on some part of the finishing of the house's interior. Dene, of course, had designed the building and drawn all its plans. I laid the ceramic tiles in the kitchen. Kim and Eric came home from their travels to put down the hardwood floor of their rooms on the second floor.

To initiate the new home officially into the family and to let it know what kind of company it had fallen in with, we lit a great pile of logs in the big kitchen fireplace, opened a last remaining bottle of wine from the harvest of '57, the year we had bought the farm, drank a long noisy series of toasts, and threw our wine glasses crashing into the roaring blaze.

Harvest was upon us, so the boys stayed to help. For the most part Dene and I did the important work ourselves, making sure that we had first made the maximum amount of experimental wines in small separate lots, then often staying up through the night crushing, destemming, and pressing the remaining grapes for sale to home winemakers. Since the service of these home winemakers often interfered with my painting schedules as well as Dene's studies, we eventually worked out an arrangement with one of the local apple processors who had refrigeration facilities. We would package our many different varieties of crushed, destemmed grapes into poly bags, which fitted into rigid waxed cardboard boxes, and take them to the processor, who would immediately freeze them solid. By this means we could schedule our activities more or less to our convenience, then send notice to all of our customers to pick up their frozen fermentable material on a single weekend. I was frustrated

by the tiny scale of my hobby winemaking but still had not
been able to convince myself or Dene that we should commit ourselves and our dandy, well-equipped little winery to
commercial operations.

However, about midsummer, with the promising harvest of 1971 approaching, we held a fateful family conference and made the decision to apply for a license to make
wine for sale, at least enough to help offset the ever-growing
cost of our hobby.

The United States Government does not charge a fee for
a winery license although it doesn't issue them casually.
There are numerous qualifications and inspections which
must be met and endured. These are more rigid than for
other types of business operations because of course the
production of all alcoholic beverages is a prime source of tax
revenue; therefore most of the regulations concern themselves with this interest more than with the wine itself. The
State of New York does charge a fee for its license, and at
that time it was a high one. Its prerequisites are equally
numerous, though generally parallel to those of the federal
government. To anyone who was as unfamiliar with the
impersonal, unfeeling, detailed rigidity of a regulatory bureaucracy as we were, the experience of applying for a winery license was chastening, to say the least. But we persev-
ered through the numerous errors on our part and rejections
on their part until at last all applications, questionnaires,
maps, floor plans, photographs, and inspections were apparently completed.

Now it was only necessary to await the arrival of our
federal permit and state license. Days passed. Weeks passed.
The federal permit didn't arrive. The state authorities agreed
to issue their license immediately upon its receipt. The
grapes were getting so ripe the birds found them irresistible,
but without our license we could not legally start making
wine. Finally the losses to birds began to be so great that we
fell back on our old techniques. We picked our ripest reds,
destemmed, packed, and took them to the cooler to be fro-

zen in the lined boxes we had used to sell to home winemakers. We pressed the whites and put the fresh juice into poly-lined fifty-five-gallon drums and had them chilled down to a temperature below fermentation level. In previous years the operator of the local cooler had been able to accommodate our fairly small amounts of grapes, and usually he only had to keep them for a few days, since our home winemaker customers arrived every weekend to buy our stock. But now our accumulation of boxes and drums was occupying so much of his refrigeration room that they were interfering with his own needs, and he warned us that he wouldn't be able to give us any more space.

I called the Bureau of Alcohol, Tobacco, and Firearms (BATF) regional office in Peekskill and was told that the license was approved and would no doubt arrive tomorrow. Eric and I decided we would have to finish picking the white grapes or lose everything to the birds. With the permit due any minute we simply had to start filling our tanks and barrels. To delay fermentation as long as possible, we sulfured the juice as heavily as we could. Two more days passed. All the white grapes were in. The weather had been beautifully sunny and warm, ideal for harvesting, but since we had no refrigeration at the winery, the warm weather also accelerated the start of yeast activity in spite of our precautions. The delicious aroma of fermenting grape juice filled the winery processing room.

About eleven o'clock the following morning we got a telephone call from the federal inspector who had been handling our application. A minor detail regarding security had been overlooked, and he would have to make one more visit as soon as he could drive up from Peekskill to measure a door opening in the very room containing the birthing wine. In spite of the fact that the inspector had been extremely courteous and helpful to us in every way he could during the application and bonding process, every horror story we had ever heard of the implacable heartlessness of the bureaucracy of alcohol control in matters of the most minor infringement of regulations flooded our minds.

Although we weren't sure, the alcohol content of our juice had very possibly reached the 2 percent level, which the regulations regarded as wine—and we had no license on the premises. Its aroma would certainly give us away. Revocation of our approval, a heavy fine, even prosecution were our probable fate. Peekskill was no more than a half hour's drive away. The inspector would be here before we could hope to move the evidence. Despairing, I sat heavily on a small drum of liquid chlorine which we had been using in a dilute solution to clean up the winery after processing. The half-empty drum turned over under my weight and spilled the cleaning solution over the floor. The fumes of chlorine were overpoweringly strong, and I started to fan them out the open door.

"Wait," Eric exclaimed, "that's it!" We hurriedly closed the doors and all windows in the room, got out a pair of wet mops, and pouring out a great quantity of the chlorine, which masked the smell of everything else, we were busily scrubbing the soaking-wet floor when the inspector and an assistant arrived. The idea had occurred to me during our anxious wait that the whole delay in the issuance of our license had been a malicious scheme just to trap us into the very position we were in, and I half expected the two men, who greeted us pleasantly as they got out of their car carrying a tape measure, to go directly to one of the juice-filled tanks, lay an ear to its side, and hear the buzzing fermentation. "Aha! just as we thought," they would say, taking handcuffs out of their pockets. But instead they went directly to the aforementioned door, quickly made the measurements they had mentioned on the phone, apologized for interrupting our work, and returned to their car. "Good luck," the inspector said as his assistant started the car. "I hope you make a million dollars." The permit arrived in the next morning's mail. I drove to New York and picked up the state license by hand that afternoon.

Even with our license and a cellar finally full of wine, we realized that our financial problems were not solved. In fact they were increased. After all, we had not decided to make wine solely for financial reasons but more to serve as a model to provide help and encouragement to others. The largest lot, or *cuvée,* of any one style of wine in the whole 2,000 gallons was perhaps 260 gallons in four of our French barrels. Most of the vintage had been made into even smaller experimental lots, each one varying in some small way, such as varietal mix, type of yeast used, choice of vineyard area, etc. It would be almost impossible to build a "custom" for such small amounts in any conventional marketing channel. Research and experimentation such as ours almost always would result in a degree of failure and reworking. Any earnings we could hope for to reward our successes would inevitably go back into future experiments.

Dene said, with pragmatic directness, "Paint more pictures." But I felt that I couldn't paint more pictures and run the farm properly too. We needed a grant, but we had already tried for that without success. Funds for an alcoholic-beverage research project were just not available in the puritanic East. Even the State Agricultural Experiment Station at

Geneva, New York, had been unable to obtain a small fund to be budgeted for wine experimentation. We considered once again the idea of opening the winery to tourists and quickly put the thought aside as totally antithetic to our purposes.

Nonetheless, it was time to sell some wine, one way or another, and that meant it had to be bottled. I called the Rabinowitz bottle people to place an order. "How many gross do you need?" I thought a moment. There were about six French barrels of Baco and a small tank of blended Seyval and Aurora. "Four hundred cases should be enough." There was a long pause at the other end of the line. Then, "You're kidding!"

"Too many?" I asked.

"Listen, mister, I haven't time to fool around. You'll have to take a hundred sixty-five gross. Minimum order."

"How much will that be?" I asked.

"Seven thousand two hundred dollars plus shipping." I had just gotten a check from London. I supposed we'd be able to use up the bottles in a few years.

"Okay." I gulped. "Send them."

About two o'clock the following afternoon an enormous trailer truck pulled into the court in front of the winery. The driver looked down at me. "Where do you want to unload?"

"Start handing them to me through that door," I said, pointing to the processing room. "I'll take them to the attic."

The driver swung down from the truck's cab and peered up the folding stairway to the small attic. "You know, I just drive this thing," he said. "I wouldn't mind helping you out for an hour or so, but . . . Ain't you got a fork lift or a set of rollers?"

I looked blank. "Uh, no."

He opened the rear doors of the massive vehicle. Cases were stacked to the ceiling from the front to the rear of the forty-five-foot trailer.

"There's maybe two thousand boxes in there," he said.

"That'd take two people a coupla days just to take it off, the way you're talkin'."

"There'll be three of us," Dene put in helpfully.

The driver ran his hand over his eyes and sighed. "Look," he said resignedly, "it's Friday. I live fairly near here, so I can take the cab off the rig and drive home. You've got the weekend to figure out how to get this stuff off."

Dene started passing the boxes to me. I carried them two at a time up the light fold-down stairway. By dark the attic was full, but the truck seemed to have hardly been touched. Two hundred and fifty trips up the fourteen steps, however, had reduced me to a panting wreck. Dene could hardly stand up after bending so often to stack the sixteen-pound boxes onto my outstretched arms. We were both barely able to get out of bed the next morning. Kim and Eric were away. We called on some local youngsters.

With the attic full we decided to fill the winery shop. Since we had no way to move the truck's trailer, this meant first loading the wine cases onto our four-wheel-drive Scout, which would hold only about twenty of them, driving it around the winery, and then unloading. With the help of our fresh young crew, by noon the shop was chock-a-block—but the truck was still over half full. The living room of our new house was not yet furnished. We stacked it to the ceiling with boxes.

At last, working hurriedly in a light drizzling rain, we removed the contents of the last fifty-ton box from the truck. Every conceivable corner of our little winery was piled high with cases of empty wine bottles. There was no room in the processing area, so bottling operations would have to take place in the cellar. Even if we could manage to bottle and sell the entire winery inventory of two thousand gallons there would not be enough room left to receive and process the next harvest.

I asked a local builder to estimate the cost of an extension large enough to replace the room now filled with empty wine bottles. "Prices have gone through the roof," he said.

"About $30,000." That would bring our total building costs alone, not including equipment, to over $65,000. And, Dene reminded me, we hadn't sold our first bottle.

Of course our friends and neighbors who had helped us pick grapes all assured us they would buy our wine when it was ready, but could they drink two thousand gallons? Counting up our really ardent and totally supportive friends —let's see, there was Ray, there were Tom, Allen, Pete, Walter—oops, no, he only drank martinis and occasionally beer. Straining my memory to list every possible friend who could be counted on to pitch in or, more accurately, "toss down" a bottle of my wine on a regular basis, it looked like each would have to consume about forty gallons a year. The national average per capita consumption at that time was less than two gallons per year.

Still there was something about the idea of making wine for friends, for a kind of expanded family, that I couldn't get off my mind. Sitting on the tractor, plowing, harrowing, spraying, all the routine activities that one does almost automatically, the drone of the tractor's engine enclosing me in a special kind of privacy that I have always found to be thought-productive, the nucleus of an idea took shape.

We would build an expanded family of serious wine-interested friends, using Benmarl's great natural beauty and the drama of her sweeping landscape to attract their support. They would not be tourists, these new friends. Surveys of other wineries had taught me that the average purchase among tourists was something less than one-quarter of a bottle per visitor. By that calculation, I would somehow have to attract, serve, and complete a sales transaction with at least forty thousand individuals just to sell the mere two thousand gallons in our cellar. Further, if one assumed that most of these people visited on weekends during the six months of peak tourist activity, I would have to cope with something like 1,538.5 visitors each weekend. Under such circumstances, Benmarl could not be the quiet wine-research-oriented experiment station we envisioned. It would become a circus!

I remembered, enviously, the dinners we had enjoyed at the old Clos de Vougeot near Nuits-St.-Georges, where my brilliant Burgundian friends met each month as the Confrérie des Chevaliers du Tastevin to dine and share with selected connoisseurs their great wines and the rich traditions of their region. Presided over by the wine producers themselves, robed in handsome medieval costume in the magnificent old monastery, great feasts served by world-famous chefs were designed to complement and dramatize their wines, which they did superbly, and the fortunate guests who participated went away with a respect for them which made them lifelong supporters of Burgundy.

That was what we needed, a way to dramatize the interesting new wines we were developing at Benmarl—wines we felt would someday be the basis for a thriving Hudson region agricultural economy.

Unfortunately we had no Clos de Vougeot or medieval traditions. But we had other things that perhaps could serve to draw attention to our work. I ticked them off on my fingers. Benmarl is the oldest surviving vineyard in the country. Its founder, Andrew Jackson Caywood, was one of the great agricultural pioneers. Its pretty little winery sits upon steep terraces looming over a lovely tranquil valley, green with vineyards and fruit trees, where America's first commercial viticulture had been born, a perfect symbol of what we hoped the valley would always remain. If we could be moved to take on such a project for the love of wine, perhaps there were others who could be persuaded to help out. After all, even though wine is in one sense just an ordinary agricultural product, a simple natural food, it is also a good deal more. It is a food of *unique* healthful and even social significance. Throughout history no other element in the human diet has been given such a respected, almost religious, importance. Not every part of the world is climatically and otherwise endowed with the environment that can produce it. Our Hudson region does have such an environment, a veritable treasure of fine fruitland!

There *must* be people, if we could only reach them, who would enjoy being patrons of the ancient art of winemaking, just as they enjoy being patrons of the opera. Perhaps there were other wine lovers whose busy daily lives would not permit them to join us in the vineyard, patiently tend a vine from the spring day it pushes out the first tiny leaf, then see it through the hazards of a long season of growth until at last its ripened grapes are pressed and the infant wine is born in the cask, but who, nonetheless, could become vicarious companions in our fascinating project. Was there deep inside the hearts of other wine lovers, as there was in ours, a

vigneron, who would like to feel the slaty vineyard soil crunch under his boots, smell the rare fragrance of the tiny grape flower, take his solitary lunch looking over the summer-green vines, wondering what his labors would produce at vintage time?

Surely there was, and if so there must be a way to share with this vicarious *vigneron* the heady satisfaction that can only come from holding the fragile stem of a wine glass, its contents limpid, fragrant, and delicious—knowing that it is absolutely unique, made from your vines, not to be purchased anywhere—yours alone.

Under the stimulus of this kind of thinking, my imagination began to conceive of a kind of private club or association of wine lovers, formed to provide support for the practical viticultural and oenological experimentation we wished to continue. I decided that we would call the organization the Société des Vignerons. Friends chide me occasionally about choosing a French name when we were and are totally dedicated to making American wine, but after all, most of our grapes are French and also I was personally saturated with an empathy for France because of our recent residence in that country. I must say that, as much as I hope to see Americans in the future produce a large part of our own wine, I feel that we owe the French a great debt of gratitude for the refinement and understanding with which they have endowed the art of winemaking, and I'm perfectly content to pay them homage.

I'm not totally sure that my family believed my idea would succeed as strongly as I did, but they gave me their support and put their energies to the task of getting the society started.

For charter members, we approached our friends who we knew shared our hopes regarding the valley, and we asked them to become vicarious grape growers: to put up a modest initiation fee to represent the cost of raising two grapevines to fruit-bearing age and to take on the financial support for these vines, which, of course, the Société would manage for them. Each pair of vines they supported would represent a symbolic unit of research and wine production, which we called a "vineright." Although no actual ownership was involved, each vineright became, in effect, their own private vineyard. For as long as they maintained their financial support in the form of an annual sponsor's fee, each vineright would provide empirical information for the advance of valley viticulture, and each was guaranteed to produce for its vicarious *vigneron* a case of wine from each succeeding vintage. This case was to be known as their "Droit de Seigneur." Each year in the spring when the wines of the previous harvest had cleared, the member *vignerons* would assemble at the winery to taste and select their *droit* from the Société's numerous wines. This wine would then be bottled under the Société's label, bearing its sponsor's signature, as the private "Cuvée du Vigneron." We also began publication of a newsletter to keep our cooperating *vignerons* in touch with their little vineyard and winery activities.

Almost immediately the response to the Société began. Our old friends were delighted with the plan. Membership grew steadily as friends brought in their friends. Even I was astonished at how quickly this plan to support the private vineyard on this historic old farm began to attract members, some wanting to learn to grow grapes and make wine, some seeking increased understanding about enjoying wines, many already connoisseurs and possessors of fine cellars and wine collections. In addition to their interest and financial support, a number of them were willing and able to help us establish, through their contacts, a credibility for our crusade to build up the old Hudson wine region, which we could not hope to accomplish alone.

The Société des Vignerons made Benmarl's idealistic goals achievable. It would be impossible for me to overstate my profound feeling of gratitude when I look back over the file of members whose purchases of vinerights provided the inspiration, the guidance, and, of course, the funds that permitted us to keep our development free from the threat of pressures to compromise quality, which are almost irresistible in the hard battle of the normal marketplace.

My mother bought the first thirty-five vinerights. No greater act of faith was ever performed. Ruby Earle-Blair-Thorp-Miller, devout Methodist, *never* knowingly drank a swallow of an alcoholic beverage in her life. She abhorred the thought of modifying the natural function of a human "God-given" brain in any way—but if her first-born son was determined to make wine—well, Christ himself had provided it for a wedding party.

Many others soon followed, including our son Eric, and in a surprisingly short time we were away! I stood with each new member personally on the edge of Benmarl's topmost terrace, talked about the valley's history, and explained our dream for its future. They returned with their friends—and soon there was no question but that they would be able and eager to consume a large amount of our wine.

Obviously I cannot name everyone who became *vignerons,* although I would love to do it and to pump each arm and kiss both cheeks in the French manner. And there are some whom I would like to single out because of the extraordinary effect they had upon Benmarl's development and, in some instances, upon the entire wine industry. I will not name them either, though I suspect they know who they are and how much I appreciate their help. One thing I learned at this

CUVÉE DU VIGNERON

Edith Caywood Meekes

time and in the months and years to come was the effective power of the press. We were able to interest a number of wine writers in what we were doing.

I'm getting ahead of my story, though, in mentioning the attention Benmarl and its Société attracted from the media for its idealistic goals and unusual way of financing them. By 1977 the value of the space and time donated to us free would have cost, if purchased, in excess of $3 million. But in the spring of 1972 there was only the *hope* of these good things to come. Always a trifle overly optimistic, I had spent our limited funds a bit lavishly and had not painted enough pictures to keep a stream of new illustrations pouring across editors' desks through my London syndicate. Art receipts were consequently low. The cellar was full of excellent wine and our steadily growing Société membership were quaffing it valiantly, but they couldn't yet drink it all,

To supplement their purchases I called on every liquor store and restaurant within a radius of seventy-five miles, walked up and down virtually every street in New York City. "Benmarl? Never heard of it." Liquor stores were a particularly tough sale. Wine meant nothing to most of them in those days.

"A fad." "The public will never go for it." "Tell ya whaddaldo," one proprietor said, lighting his well-chewed cigar and puffing in my face as he leaned conspiratorially toward me, "Gimme one on tree and you godda sale."

"What's one on three?" I asked innocently.

"Come on, whaddayus some kind of a hick? I order tree, ya deliver me four."

"No thanks."

The contrast between my two ways of life was laughable. The previous summer on a junket to Norway, the publisher of my art work, Per Mortensen, had taken me to lunch at the Royal Yacht Club. The famous sailor-king was dining alone at his table and smiled pleasantly at us as we passed him. The chef had paid his respects first to the king and then stopped to chat with us at Per's table, making me promise to bring him some of my American wine on my next visit. Now I was lucky to be able to get my sales pitch completed before an impatient New York restaurateur would interrupt, "Sorry, my wine list is already printed," and he would walk away.

In spite of the rude rebuffs, I found myself enjoying the challenge. The third time I called on my cigar-chewing liquor-store operator he laughed when he saw me coming, "Okay, bub. Send me five boxes. If I can't sell it I'll drink it myself."

There were some wonderfully nice people among the rough ones. I walked into a charming little shop on Forty-ninth Street near Lexington one morning. It appeared tiny but its shelves were lined with wines—good wines. The pleasant man and woman behind the counter listened to my story patiently, even asking interested questions. "Could you bring us twenty cases?" they asked when I had finished. Could I! It was my biggest sale yet. "Your billing name?" I asked. "Morrell's." They have been one of my best customers ever since and their success in bringing their son Peter into their business and growing to become one of the best wine shops in the world has brought me enormous pleasure.

Sam Aaron at Sherry-Lehmann's, then Sherry's, also was one of those adventurous wine merchants who gave me an order, and his shop has never been without Benmarl since the first purchase. Sam and his close friend actor Burgess Meredith even became involved later in my work to expand Hudson Region wine-grape-growing by appearing and speaking at a growers' conference. They brought with them a delightfully charming man, the Marquis de Roussy de Sales. François, as he asked to be called, was a top executive and stockholder in the vast firm of Christian Dior, which owns a great amount of wine property, and he and his wife were personally the owners of the enormous Château de La Chaize, the largest producer in the Brouilly region of Beaujolais. His excellent wine sold well in America. He spoke eloquently and convincingly at our conference. Although a titled Frenchman, he had received part of his education in America at Harvard and spoke English without a trace of French accent, which has always slightly dampened the retelling of my favorite story of his visit to Benmarl. We were in the cellar and I had just pipetted a large splash of our new 1973 Baco-Foch blend of red wine into his glass. He sniffed and examined the wine's color, holding it against Sam's white shirt, then tasted tentatively. "Excellent!" he exclaimed, genuinely shocked with pleased surprise. "Absolutely splendid!" I beamed. "If I had met this wine anywhere else, without your assurance that it was grown on this property," he went on, "I would have assumed immediately that it was a first-rate Beaujolais—not mine, you understand, but Pierre's, just next door." We all laughed at this droll compliment.

"Just like a Frenchman," teased Meredith, "pulling the rug out from under his praise with the last few words."

I confess, François, if you should ever read this, that even today I often tell this story of your visit and your remarks, as an example of Gallic humor, but I overlook your flawless English and quote you as speaking with a heavy French accent.

François has remained a friend to me and has also exerted a constant influence toward the betterment of French wine. He once asked Sam Aaron to send him "some of Mark's wine" in order to show French growers that laissez-faire is dangerous. American technology was excellent and soon eastern American wines would be a competitive force in the world market.

chapter VIII

A Misstep

Between the arduous sales trips I spent my time farming. Neither of the boys was available on a regular basis. Song writing, guitar playing, and traveling were far more fascinating than mounting a tractor at daybreak or hand-hoeing the weeds, which seemed to leap out of the ground the minute I left the farm to sell wine. Even our small vineyard was more than one man could handle alone, but revenues were not yet adequate to hire a competent assistant. My studio was still set up for painting, but there was no time for it.

One rainy morning, too wet for my planned vineyard work, I sat down in the old chair I had been using to paint from for more than thirty-five years. There was an unfinished picture on my drawing board, untouched for almost a year. I picked up a brush and started to wet it. It slipped clumsily out of my fingers. I looked at my callused, blistered, work-hardened hands, too stiff to hold a brush. "Gentleman's game indeed!" I sighed. Roland should have added, ". . . and a peasant's art."

Frank Kernan entered Benmarl's history at just about that point. He and a friend had experimented with grape growing on a small scale. His friend's interest in wine had in fact led him into an interest in wine investment in France. One day, lunching at the nearby Bird and Bottle Inn, they had tasted Benmarl wine and liked it. Curious, they asked the proprietor for directions and came to visit me. Both seemed to be very pleased by what they found. Since they both seemed interested, I talked to them at some length about my plans for Benmarl and for the redevelopment of vineyards in the whole Hudson region. Frank became a member directly and set out to help Benmarl by spreading the gospel of its good work.

A short time later the friend returned with somewhat more complex plans, also intended to help Benmarl. I was very attracted to his ideas. I had had very little success in persuading local farmers to spend the money for planting wine grapes. He instead proposed to attract outside investors to provide the financing for vineyard development in return for the substantial tax benefits that were then available to agricultural ventures. This was the method of financing, he pointed out, that made California's recent spurt of grape planting possible. The plan involved raising what seemed to me very large sums of money, which would be used for the purchase of land, the cost of planting grapes, a limited expansion of Benmarl's own vineyard and its wine-production facilities, and the eventual construction of a large winery. Because the project, as he envisioned it, was so much more grandiose than I had ever allowed myself to imagine, I was very skeptical at first, but I was finally persuaded. Together with a third partner, we began to assemble a detailed projection of the total venture's operation. We named it Vineyard Development Incorporated (VDI). I was to handle land se-

lection, viticultural operations, and winemaking. My partners would handle the financing.

For me it seemed an almost miraculous opportunity to
speed up my plodding efforts to redevelop a major viticultural industry in the valley. I knew exactly which properties
we would need to obtain. One of them, the Hampton estate,
became available before VDI was in a position to buy. I
bought it myself to lease to the company. VDI then bought
a magnificent hundred-acre hillside known in the area as
Mt. Zion. We would terrace and plant its lower eastern
slopes, and on its crest, standing twelve hundred feet above
the valley floor, commanding an incredible view of thousands of acres of farmland, we planned eventually to build
a 500,000-gallon winery and reception facility, which would
surely be the most beautiful in the world.

For the first time I was able to offer a reasonable salary
for help, and I set out to build a farm and winery management team. Dene and I knew that Eric had a superior winemaking talent as well as personality traits which could make
him an outstanding executive as the company grew. He had
already helped a lot with getting our business started but
kept drifting off to other activities. He was a good musician
and like all youngsters of his day wanted to be a rock star.
With a dependable salary to offer I persuaded him to come
back from his wanderings and take a management role in the
new business.

The job we had before us was a particularly tricky one.
The number of vines we calculated we would plant on the
various properties that were owned or contracted to produce
for the company amounted to only about 52,000, which
would require the equivalent of a little more than 86 acres
on flat land. But the terrains they would be planted on were
mostly hillsides, ranging in steepness from 5 to 25 percent,
and had to be literally carved into terraces in order for modern farm machinery to be employed in their management.
Consequently, the actual amount of land that had to be dealt

with to obtain the equivalent of 86 acres of flat vineyard was 196 acres, including Benmarl. The disproportion between the acreage bought to be stripped of old orchards and the amount of it that could eventually be planted with vines was great for a number of reasons, but we had carefully considered the economic implications of the situation. Our first measure of land suitability was its microclimate. Although the Hudson region, because of its long use as agricultural land, had probably the best-recorded climate conditions of any region in the United States, its infinitely varied terrain created small pockets of special climatic character, which could critically affect the ripening of grapes. All of our planned planting zones represented superior locations.

The second measure was the character of the soil. All were well-drained, Taconic Province parcels, perfect for grapes. The third requirement was that our land be dramatically beautiful, and it was this quality that provided us with the rationale for paying out more in development as well as acquisition and mortgage costs for these beginning parcels than would normally have been required. These lands were to be the prototype, the symbolic representation, the inspiration for all the development of the future Hudson region wine district! If these rugged sites could be made to succeed, we could then go on to develop thousands of other acres—perhaps less handsome, but easier to work—that would provide the volumes of grapes needed.

The first priority was to rebuild those vineyards of Benmarl that had been too steep or, for one reason or another, too difficult to renovate with the simple tools available to Milton and me. They were planted with various of Caywood's exotic crossbred varieties, mostly genetic variations of the Delaware grape. Even though they had supplied us with the raw materials for most of the wine that had kept our amateur spirits high in our first few years, they must now be replaced with varieties suitable for the more subtle wines we could now create. Their site had serious erosion problems as well. The layout of the rows had been dictated

in the 1800s by the shale outcroppings, running generally
north and south, forcing the early vineyards to be planted
parallel to and between them. The rows were so steep that
during more than 150 years of cultivation most of the topsoil
had washed down and now lay at their base, where the vines
flourished. But at their tops the barren sterile shale could
support little or no vine growth. During the years of our
absence they had grown up in dense brush and poison ivy.

I went back to Fred Robinson, my friendly banker, for
advice as to who was the best bulldozer operator. "Jimmy
and Bob LaPolla have a big machine that ought to do your
job," he said. The next morning at daybreak Bob met me on
the hill at Benmarl and I explained what we needed to do:
cut a series of curving terraces, a minimum of nine feet wide,
hugging the hillside—right across the ancient jutting shale
outcroppings, which had for centuries dictated the shape of
all Hudson region farms. "Can you do it?" I asked.

Bob walked away from me without answering. I followed, clambering up and over the outcroppings as he paced
off their length, squinting against the rising sun to estimate
their height.

"The soil conservation fellows recommend we start cutting here and run a terrace to there with a drop of one foot
in twenty-five for best erosion control," I said.

He grunted noncommittally. "It'll cost ya," he said
finally, kicking at a point of shale with his boot. He picked
up the chunk he had dislodged. "This is easy. Water gets in
between the layers"—he ran his finger along the grain of the
shale—"and frost breaks it up, but anywhere we cut in past
the frost line it'll be hard. When it gets too hard we'll have
to go around, or up, or somewhere, no matter what the
conservation boys say. It'll take time, and time with my
machine is twenty-five an hour." I flinched. "It ain't gonna
be easy," he said.

"But can you do it?" I pressed.

"I can do it."

That evening his big D-8 tractor with an eight-foot

blade on the front and a ripping tooth on the back was unloaded on the site, and the next morning at dawn we set out a series of small flags diagonally across the face of the hill, using a transit to plot our intended grade. Now the hard part would be to hold that grade as we made our first cut. With luck the frost-rotted shale would crumble easily in front of the dozer's slanting blade and, mixing with the topsoil, fall away from the blade's trailing edge on the hill's down side, forming a perfect loose-textured "windrow" of soil to plant in. We worked from flag to flag, cutting, backing, cutting again, filling, slowly building a firmly-packed shelf, which followed the horizontal curve of the hill as closely as possible. In a little over an hour's time we reached the last flag. Terrace number one: almost 450 feet long, it would hold approximately 70 grapevines. It had been a relatively easy cut, but we didn't know that then. Neither did we know with any precision how many more such vine spaces we could make the old hill yield. Five weeks later we did.

Benmarl, that stubborn, stony old lady had forced us to change our course dozens of times, to go around many unyielding outcrops we had hoped to cut off. Our ideal grade had also been compromised in many places. But in the end we had carved out eleven miles of new vineyard rows, wide enough to accommodate a truck, and created planting space for 7,000 new vines, bringing Benmarl's total to 9,500, permitting a sizable increase of our Pinot Noir, Chelois, Cabernet Sauvignon, Chancellor, de Chaunac, Seyval and Chardonnay vineyards.

It was too late in the season to obtain and plant vines, so we seeded the terraces on the top sides and the terrace walls with grass to prevent erosion. Along the three-foot planting zone at the crest of each terrace we applied a light spray of Karmex to discourage weed growth. Roundup would have been better but it wasn't available then in the United States.

Our oldest son, Kim, who had never had as much interest in the vineyard as Eric, was living with a friend in an old house sitting right on the edge of the Hudson River in a nearby town. The house had been a part of an old sawmill, the rusted remains of which were still in place, as if waiting for someone to crank up the ancient one-cylinder engine that had powered it. Kim was fascinated by the mill. He seemed to enjoy having me come to look at the machinery with him as if somehow he was hoping that our combined imaginations could give the ancient hulk a new reason for being—as we were doing for Benmarl. The fantasy was almost palpable as we turned the massive creaking saw blade and reconstructed, in an animated conversation, the way it must have been in its heyday.

Kim had always liked to work with wood. I remembered another similar occasion. He couldn't have been more than four years old. When I had time to play with him, which my intensely demanding art career made regrettably rare, he liked for us to build things. That morning we were busily nailing some boards together. It was to be an airplane, we said, just to give the project a name, although the fun of being together and banging noisily away with our hammers while we laughed and chatted was really enough of a reason. Kim was getting very good at driving nails. He drove a long spike through four short pieces of light planking. When he turned them over to bend down the nail point the boards turned on the pivot of the spike, fanning out like spokes on an axle. "Look!" Kim shouted, holding the splayed boards over his head. "Our airplane is a helicopter." We banged away more purposefully until we were tired and decided that we were finished; then we stepped back to look at our creation.

"Dad," Kim said, "I'm glad we're not rich."

"Why?" I asked surprised.

"So we have to build our own helicopters!" he replied. I picked him up and threw him, laughing, over my shoulder, and we went inside.

I pricked my finger slightly on the tooth of the old blade

and the memory faded. "Kim," I said, "we're going to need more than eight thousand new grape posts to build trellises for Benmarl's new vineyards. If you could supply them I can now afford to buy them." He, of course, knew what was involved. He had often gone into our woodlot with Milton and me to cut down black locust trees, whose wood is extremely resistant to rot. Felled, the tree would be cut into nine-foot lengths, then split with steel wedges into posts on the spot. In spite of its hardness the locust grows rapidly, and the local woods around Marlboro were full of large trees, each of which would yield as many as a dozen fine grape posts. Logging roads would have to be cut deep into the woods to get to the best trees. It would be a hard, lonely, dangerous job but if anyone could do it Kim could. "Could I work as an independent contractor?" he asked.

"Sure," I replied.

"I'll think about it," he hedged.

But I had seen an adventurous light go on in his eye. Both stray lambs were now back in the fold.

Bob and I moved the dozing operations to Mt. Zion, which presented a much more complex terracing problem, but by this time we were experts. I knew that he could make his big machine work as efficiently as could be expected. It was no longer necessary for me to ride with him. He knew by this time what I needed and what kinds of compromises were acceptable. With someone to serve as his flagman he could work without my constant direction.

Meanwhile, the second part of VDI's financing plan, finding a major investor to put up the capital to buy and plant additional land as well as build the winery on Mt. Zion, had not met with instant success, and although it was too early to be discouraged, the earlier optimism my partners and I had originally felt took on a quieter determination. They had splendid business connections. All potential investors were brought to Benmarl by the dozens, to dine, to taste the wines, and to inspect the properties being developed as vineyards. We made an impressive showing on a micro-scale of what we proposed to achieve on a macro-scale. Our guests were toured through Benmarl's modest though efficient winery, then served its young but already quite elegant wines with a luncheon designed to complement them, prepared and served by Dene and Margaret Schramm. While dining they looked out over Benmarl's producing estate vineyards down to the new terraces now being trellised with Kim's posts. After lunch we habitually drove them past the Hampton estate, which had been a thriving tree-fruit farm and was now being cleared of its trees in preparation for terracing. Then to climax our presentation we had cut a broad road across the crest of Mt. Zion to the proposed site of our future winery. Standing there looking out beyond Bob's big machine below, combing miles of terraced vineyards into its southeastern slopes, we looked over thousands of acres of the best and richest fruitland of America to the flashing ribbon of the Hudson River. It was impossible for our guests not to see the vision of the vast potential wine industry that had been imprinted on my brain for almost all the fifteen years I had lived in this valley.

Mt. Zion was finished. It and Benmarl were planted. Bob moved to Hampton and finished the rough terracing. I moved our planting crew in behind him. John Pizzo, a friend and local farmer, with his three uncles, the Zambito brothers, had joined us during the planting of Zion, and we had developed a technique for planting steep terraces by cutting a furrow with a tooth mounted on an outrig carried by our small Ferguson D-2 bulldozer. The vines were simply set at intervals in the furrow, though sometimes Milton's old podger was put to use again to deepen the planting holes in rocky spots, and then their roots were covered by a pass with the grape hoe on our regular farm tractor.

As the year of '74 proceeded, our efforts to obtain large-scale financing took place against a darkening cloud of pessimism about wine investment in general. A misrepresentation by a large French wine producer as to the source of some of its wines had caused a terrible scandal in France. It was astonishing how an unrelated event of that sort could dampen the enthusiasm of our investors. There was no logical reason for it to do so but it did. I was reminded of the droll comment made by one of my London editors at the time of an earlier similar scandal in England: "When one can't be sure that one man's fourteen-guinea Nuits-St.-Georges is not the same as another man's twenty-shilling Beaujolais, one just orders a pint of stout instead!"

From inside the wine business we saw the problem as only a momentary "overbite" by a growing infant industry. America's healthy appetite for wine would quickly digest it. This proved to be the case. A great deal of credit is given to the management of the Bank of America for its calm refusal to panic as loans came up for payment, which the low price of grapes would not provide. Mortgages and development loans were extended. The quality of jug wines rose noticeably for a time, but the long-term forward thrust of the California wine industry was hardly more disturbed than a burp would upset a nursing baby.

Ironically, VDI was hurt. This was no time to be trying to raise large amounts of money, as we were, for a wine venture anywhere.

Finally, in order to avoid what appeared to be severe financial hazards ahead, Dene and I decided to withdraw from VDI by personally borrowing sufficient money to repay the corporation for investments it had made in Benmarl. This allowed us to arrange an amicable dissolution of our association.

Both Eric and Kim were now deeply involved and seemed to identify their future with Benmarl. With the vintage of '75 coming up, Eric was preparing to take over the winemaking and Kim was now willing to accept the title of Vineyard Manager.

Our backs were to the wall financially but it was not an unfamiliar position. Crisis and lack of money had almost always been the way of life for Benmarl. The important thing was that we, the family, would defend the ramparts together. It would have been great for VDI to succeed; the development of a Hudson wine region could have been light years ahead. But it had not succeeded, so here we were, and the job was still to be done.

I assessed our position. Benmarl's home vineyards were in excellent condition, fully planted and thriving. We had adequate farm equipment. The vintage approaching promised to be an excellent one. The winery's capacity was now approximately 16,000 gallons, about half of which was presently filled with previous vintages in one stage or another, bottled, in barrel, or in tank. This would permit us to produce about 8,000 gallons of new wine. We would have approximately the same amount, theoretically, to sell during the coming year. If we assumed the total sale of that amount at our current average case price, we would take in a gross sum of about $100,000. "Well, now, that's a respectable

figure," I thought. "We should be able to get by." I realized uneasily, however, that I was not an experienced business-man. I had earned our living entirely as an artist. Terms such as "capital expenditure" translated into the purchase of a few brushes a year and a tube or so of paint, "long-term debt" a small mortgage maybe.

The fact was that Benmarl had always been . . . what was the term Roland had used? There isn't really a word in the French language for what we think of as "hobby." The expression Roland had used had come about because the well-known French painter Dominique Ingres was reputed to be passionately addicted to playing the violin—so much so that he was thought by his friends to neglect his profes-sional work. Because of this it became fashionable to refer to one's avocational interests as *un violon d'Ingres.*

Benmarl had, up to now, been *mon violon.* It had never, to this point, been asked to pay its own total expenses, much less to make us a living.

I was pretty sure I could sell the 8,000 gallons; that would work out to be about 3,300 cases. I subtracted all the operating expenses I could think of from the $100,000; that left $26,100.52—not enough to pay the interest and princi-pal on our debts. I hadn't included any salary for Dene or me but I had tried to leave the boys' incomes at the same level they had been when they were employed by VDI. We could provide them both with housing. Eric would stay on in the small apartment above the barn. Kim had recently married so we could install him with Mary, his new bride, in the Hampton estate cottage—not exactly a palace but adequate. The question we had to put to them was, could they accept a smaller cash payment on the grounds that the business would pay all shelter expenses? They gamely agreed to try. At last, by shaving a figure here and cutting another there I arrived at a nearly balanced outflow and income for Benmarl.

However, there were no funds in this budget for finish-ing the development of the Hampton estate vineyards. We, of course, had been left with the combined mortgages for both the parcels that comprised it, the one Dene and I had hastily bought for the convenience of VDI and a smaller one that we had put in Eric's name when we felt assured that its mortgage and development costs were secured by VDI. Now, both mortgages were totally our problem, as well as the interest and repayment of their development loans.

chapter IX

A Little Help from Our Friends

There was no possibility of selling Hampton for the same familiar reason I had met before: more was invested in it than it was worth in its present unfinished state. Also we needed it. Desperately. My calculations had just proved that Benmarl's present production of 8,000 gallons a year simply couldn't make a living for three families. Our business had to grow. Hampton, fully matured, could double our wine production and presumably make us profitable. There was only one hitch. Where would we get the $90,000 it would take to finish its vineyards and carry its operating expenses until it could become productive. It looked like a hopeless problem.

A number of the investors in the VDI venture had become members of the Société des Vignerons, which had not been a part of the company. Even though they could see that there was little hope that any investment in VDI would be recoverable, they understood that its failure was not my fault. In fact they would be willing to contribute financing to my ongoing operation if I could offer them a plan to invest in. One of these, Joe Lee, whom both Dene and I had already come to like immensely, handed me a check and said, "Put it to work. If it ever earns anything you can pay me back, but don't worry about that." Frank Kernan had never been drawn into VDI's seed financing. "Don't like the deal," he said from the first. That should have told me something then but it hadn't. Now, however, with Benmarl's future in serious jeopardy, he persuaded his mother, Maud Kernan, to back our new venture, and he "threw in what he could" himself.

With a little over a third of the $90,000 needed for Hampton already in hand, I began to form a crude idea for an investment plan that could accept the offered funds and also raise the difference. I took it to Joe Lee for advice. He arranged for me to have a luncheon meeting with a few of his friends who were investment bankers. My plan took on a little more shape. They showed me that the modest profits I forecast for Hampton would not attract a sophisticated investor. There would have to be some tax benefits. I called in the young lawyer who had helped me with VDI. He, with Joe Lee to provide the investment expertise and me to project the agricultural input, drafted a limited partnership, which provided an early return of capital contributions through tax write-offs for high-bracket investors and a fair income through a higher-than-average interest rate to others. It was, at best, clearly a high-risk proposition. "Do you think it will succeed?" I asked Joe. "You'll know who your friends are if it does," he admitted, laughing wryly. "But, Joe, I'll work my tail off to make that a great vineyard," I said.

"I know you will, Mark. That's why you have my money."

A few weeks later twenty-two friends had put their money on the line as well.

I couldn't conceal my satisfaction in having created an investment vehicle and seen it successfully subscribed. I had also learned an important lesson for anyone seriously interested in developing a successful wine business—the necessity of understanding about tax shelters, tax laws, real-estate values, and other practical money matters. It was the beginning of a new kind of role for me. Benmarl was now a full-fledged business, responsible to others as well as the family. Someone had to learn how to run it. I bought books on management and on accounting. I enrolled in a night course, Basic Business Principles. When the tractors rolled out to the vineyards past my office window in the mornings I looked ruefully after them. More and more this desk would be my place. Not exactly what I had planned.

The spring of '76 was a textbook example of Hudson region climate. By mid-February, following a short but fairly intense cold period just after Christmas, we had the usual early thaw. Marlboro lies low between the forty-first and forty-second parallels of the globe. The eastern and southern slopes of the Hudson Valley were bathed in the same bright sunshine that six hours earlier had melted snow on Caesar's Forum and stirred the dormant buds in vineyards surrounding Rome. It would be only a brief warming here, however. Repeated invasions of chilled air from Canada would intermittently interrupt the warming trend before Hudson region grape buds would shift into a growing mode. The deep, cold waters of the great river itself play an important part in the timing of that event, keeping the ambient air temperatures down just to the dormancy threshold in spite of the bright sunshine.

Eric and Kim laid aside cellar work to enjoy the few days of warmth and begin the season's pruning. Snow was two feet thick in the Foch vineyards just outside my office and covered the lower trunks of the vines, but the upper parts of the trellis were free of snow so that the major part of the pruning could be accomplished. Later, less skilled hands could remove any lower canes.

Standing on the small balcony behind my desk, looking up the rows of the adjoining vineyard, I could see the canes of the previous year's growth draw a pattern of brown lines against the background of snow, each rising from the cordon wrapped along the trellis wire, then falling in a slow curve toward the vineyard floor, forming the impression of a giant skeleton of a rib cage. We had often called it the "whale," but from where I stood today it appeared long and slightly undulating—more like an eel.

The boys were breaking in new pruners and had chosen to start them on the cordon-trained vines because the pruning principle was so simple. The new cane growth of the previous season was easy to identify by its size and bright brown color. The pruner only had to be taught to leave a short spur of two buds nearest the cordon. One of the new pruners was very short and had to reach over his head to snip off the canes. Watching him reminded me of Charlie Castrogiovanni, a neighboring apple farmer who loved wine and who had, for a number of years, helped me prune Benmarl's vines when Dene and I were managing the vineyards alone. He had overcome the same problem by pruning with long lopping shears, and to give himself a few inches of extra reach he would often stand on the raised berm under the trellis inside the "rib cage," pruning from the inside out, "in the belly of the whale" we joked. For a number of years Charlie and I worked together, when he could find the time. We never talked very much and we almost never saw each other except in pruning season, but there was a warm feeling of friendship between us. He died unexpectedly a couple of years ago and I have missed him severely ever since.

When the weather began to get really warm around mid-March Charlie would often sing while he worked: "O Sole Mio," "Cella Luna," etc. He had a naturally good but

untrained voice with a flair for drama, which made him sound better, perhaps, than he really was. I'm sure I heard him at his best one day in the highest rear portion of the Baco vineyard. There in the winter one can stand and look up the valley almost to the Newburgh narrows, an inspiring view—especially under a Hudson region sky, such as we had that day. Charlie and I had been pruning for a number of hours, and since he was faster than I he was working some distance away from me. The bright spring sun would peep out periodically from flocks of fleecy clouds running fast across the sky before a Canadian high jet, which didn't affect the air at ground level. When the sun shone between clouds the still air was hot, and a few moments of it would make one shed one's coat.

Charlie had been singing animatedly as he worked. Suddenly he stopped as a shaft of sunlight shot through a break in the clouds and transformed the valley into a stage, lighting the ochre bluffs of Quarry Hill, turning them into a brilliant gold against the dark bluish-purple hills across the river. As we watched, another shaft spotlighted the red-tiled roof of the monastery, topping the purple hill with a blazing jewel. There was no sound. It was as if the lights were building suspense for a dramatic scene in an opera. In a moment the actor would appear and the climactic action would unfold. A third light shaft fell upon Charlie. He looked up at the sky as if he had been called, then threw his arms open, holding his pruning loppers as if they were a sword, and burst into the heart-rending aria from *Pagliacci,* singing toward the dark hills as if they were the ranked armchairs of La Scala.

Presently the light moved and the magic illusion passed also. Charlie faltered, forgetting the words, and fell silent. His arms dropped. He turned, remembering he had an audience, smiled at me embarrassed, lifted his arms, and turned his palms toward me in a gesture half bow and half shrug, then turned back to his work. Bravo, Charlie, bravo . . .

As we moved into 1976, if the future of Benmarl as a

business venture was still uncertain its success as a producer of astonishingly good wines was not. Along with Konstantin Frank's Vinifera Cellars and Walter Taylor's Bully Hill, the Miller family's Benmarl had demonstrated an understanding of the subtleties of the art of winemaking which was a total surprise to the majority of wine-conscious people. Its clean, fresh, totally dry white wines, made largely from the Seyval Blanc grape, barrel-aged for six to ten months in French oak from the Nevers forest (or for similar periods in various other oaks from American forests), were sheer vinous poetry. With the spicy, tantalizingly delicious young reds, blended of Baco Noir, Chelois and Maréchal Foch grapes, given the same barrel storage, they clearly offered the kind of use potential that one would previously have had to look for in fine French wines.

These were the products, I felt, of the family's intimate understanding of the traditions of Burgundian winemakers. The labor of making them, though, was more and more Eric's. He knew he was succeeding and that awareness pushed him to run his crew on twenty-four-hour schedules during harvest season. It was an enormous satisfaction for me to see his commitment to winemaking and to Benmarl. In spite of the hectic pace, the heady aroma of fermenting grape juice seemed to have the power to inspire him to heroic effort and endurance of the long hours. I would walk over to the winery at 4 A.M., after being wakened by the noise of the tractor running past my window to dump press pomace, and find him and his crew in a gay bacchanalian mood. He would hold up a test tube of grape juice being checked for sugar content. "Twenty-three brix," he would say, grinning. I had to chuckle. There he stood, streaky-faced, purple-armed, and red-eyed, obviously exhausted but merry as a young satyr bludgeoned by bosoms or smothered with kisses. The charm of his young wines was nicely complemented by the older wines, which Dene and I had made in the years before. These, even with only four years of bottle age, were developing a kind of heady aroma and

lightly toasted flavor, very Burgundian in character, which no one had ever been known to achieve west of the Atlantic.

The contrast between the wines of these small wineries, using only New York–grown grapes, and those of the big established New York wineries, which mixed California wines with those they made from the standard juice and jelly grapes of the Finger Lake region, was ridiculous. Because they made dull wines, or perhaps more aptly, because of the poor sales of dull wines, the big wineries were not buying the full production of New York grape growers. This was resulting in a depressed grape market, which threatened to ruin the New York grape industry. Apparently the resistance shown earlier by grape growers to the idea of farm wineries disappeared in the face of this threat. The newly elected administration of Governor Hugh Carey installed John Dyson as the Commissioner of the Department of Agriculture and Markets. Dyson was interested in wine and realized that its increased production could be important to the state's economy. A bill permitting farm wine production which had failed to get beyond committee consideration during the previous legislative session (probably for the same reasons mine had failed) was revived. A task force committee headed by Assemblyman Daniel Walsh was created to assess the value of this idea and the amount of support behind it.

I was tremendously excited by these events and decided to do all I could to see that this opportunity to change New York's retarded wine industry was not lost again. I was no political strategist, but experience had taught me that, unless there was a strong public awareness of an issue of this sort, it would be quite possible for the assemblymen and senators who would eventually have to vote on the matter to be persuaded by a powerful opposing lobbying effort to let the whole idea die in committee again.

I asked to be allowed to testify before the task force's hearing in New York and I wrote to Frank Prial at the *New York Times,* inviting him to attend the hearing, hoping he would help to publicize the farm-winery concept. I also sent him a copy of my testimony, which reviewed our, at that time, twenty years of successful experience in growing and making wine of grapes grown in the Hudson Valley and urged support of legislation which would make it easy for other farmers to do as we and the very limited number of other similar small wine producers had done. These little wineries had attracted the attention of wine connoisseurs everywhere. Their achievement could be multiplied by hundreds with the encouragement of relaxed regulations and lower license fees. I urged the legislators to dispose of the out-of-date regulations that were stifling a potentially great new industry and outlined a five-point program of what I felt should be the salient objectives of farm-winery legislation.

After I had made my testimony, Chairman Walsh thanked me politely and I drove home feeling vaguely embarrassed that I had let myself get wound up in my old sermon once again. Prial had not been able to come. How could it succeed? The big wineries would simply speak to their representatives and no affirmative action would be taken. Who would apply for the farm license even if such a thing were created? Probably not Walter Taylor. He was already too well established to need it, although he had been a supporter of it. The same was true of Konstantin Frank. Crosby was selling High Tor. Even Benmarl was strong enough now to survive without it. No one I knew had actually shown much interest in the idea recently.

Although Mr. Prial did not attend the farm-winery hearing, he did discuss the subject favorably in his column, Wine Talk, and his comments undoubtedly drew attention to the concept. Surprisingly, after the task force committee had finished its information-gathering tour in January a bill was introduced in February in the State Assembly, which proposed four of the five points I had recommended. This quick action clearly indicated that there was more general support for the idea than I had dared to hope. But I curbed my burst of optimism. It would be tougher to get action in the Senate. Surprisingly again, everything went well. I persuaded my own state senator to help sponsor it, and by March a senate bill co-sponsored by Senators Hudson, Schermerhorn, Mason, and Present was presented and passed.

On June 4, 1976, Governor Carey signed the farm-winery bill into law, during a short ceremony which all twelve of the legislative sponsors attended. But only four winemakers and one nonlicensed grape grower attended. Not a very auspicious show of support for what I had been touting as "the opening of a new era in New York viticultural history." Governor Carey, however, was magnificent in his praise for the achievement. He warmly thanked Walter Taylor for the symbolic gift of a young vine pulled from his vineyard. He graciously accepted samples of their wine from Fred Johnson and Ray Knafo (representing Boordy Vineyards) and eloquently received my offering of an honorary membership in the Société des Vignerons, saying that he had, only the week before, shared a bottle of Benmarl's wine with a fellow Société member, Ambassador to Ireland Walter Curley, at the embassy in Dublin.

I was concerned that, after all the stir, to which I had contributed, to create the opportunity for farmers to become winemakers, there might, after all, be no one interested. I decided that I *must,* in recognition of the splendid effort on the part of all who had made it possible, apply for permission to relicense Benmarl as a farm winery. I was relieved to learn from a telephone call to the State Liquor Authority that three other applications had also been received and that I would be issued Farm Winery License number one in recognition of my work to foster its creation. Less than eight years later the number of similar licenses issued or pending would be approaching eighty.

As a result of news reports about the bill and my role in it our mail became massive. The membership of the Société doubled in a few days' time. Grape growers telephoned and wrote to us from everywhere, asking for guidance in creating farm wineries. By the end of 1976 the new type of farmer winemakers outnumbered, by more than twice, the number of old-style New York wineries. As a result of the stories about us and other vineyards, curiosity about winemaking as a profession and as an alternate lifestyle proliferated and also, apparently, gave confidence to government officials to recognize the new wineries publicly. Governor Carey, in a speech, warned, "California, look out!" Lieutenant Governor Krupsak went on a highly publicized personal tour of the wineries of the state. The Department of Agriculture and Markets published a guide to the state's wineries and also a handsome poster blazoned "New York State Wines, They've Come of Age!" The *New York Times* continued to give space to farm wineries. *Time* magazine published a full-color story not only discussing Benmarl, but also describing the successes of the many other entrepreneurial vineyards and wineries springing up all over eastern America. They were "Shaking California's Throne!", *Time* headlined its article. These stories gave a legitimacy to the subject, which had more often than not been treated as a whimsical fad. Now, however, if the struggles of a few small winemakers to change the public impression that all wines made east of California were some sort of sweet liquefied concord grape jelly were important enough for major media to cover, then there must be some substance to their effort. Soon, virtually every magazine in the country had published, or was in the process of researching, a feature story on New York or eastern wine. The curtain had been raised on the drama of the birth of a new industry.

As the new wineries blossomed, their proprietors were, at first, people we knew. Most had visited Benmarl during their decision-making period to discuss grape varieties they might plant (we grew or had grown somewhere near seventy-five different varieties in our long experimental years) and to taste the wines made from them. Benmarl served as a model, or perhaps in some cases an anti-model, for many of them. But by the second year after the passage of the farm-winery legislation there was an even more epidemic surge of new, or intended, licensees whom we had never met. Some of these did not, in fact, know anyone in the wine or vineyard business. They had simply "had the call" as old-time evangelists used to say. Many of them searched us out because of the extensive publicity we had received. Some traveled long distances to visit us. The variety of their character fascinated me. They ranged from sandal-shod prep-school dropouts searching for a romantic self-image to middle-aged successful men and women, bored with the usual popular pleasures of affluence, looking for some earthier, more fundamental satisfaction. Some we could help; some we couldn't. In every case we gave them freely of our time to discuss everything from how to set a vineyard post to where to find a wine press. If they lived reasonably close to us we went to visit and help assess their potential vineyard site. Although there was a certain egotistical satisfaction in it, our free advisory service began to interfere seriously with our own work. I was intensely involved in learning how to manage our expanding business and Eric was equally occupied in running its operations. However, the memory of the willing assistance that had been given to us by Philip Wagner and Everett Crosby in our own beginning days made it impossible for us to turn down any reasonable request for help.

The demand for advice extended to all hours of the day and night. I dreaded the sound of the telephone bell during meals as it so often heralded a long discussion of what to do about an unyielding epidemic of powdery mildew or a stuck fermentation. Dene learned to recognize the early symptoms of these protracted conferences by the fact that after the first greeting words I would lapse into long periods of listening. She would turn to me, lifted eyebrows asking the silent question, and I would confirm the dreaded truth with an uplifted open palm and a helpless shrug. She would proceed to dine alone, frequently to finish and wash the dishes, then retire to bed or to read before I could get back to a cold plate. Worse were the late-night calls. Startled from an exhausted sleep, my tired "hello" would occasionally prompt an apologetic offer to call back the next day. But by then I would be awake—and would often remain awake for hours after the caller's questions had been answered, wondering if I had said the right things.

Generally the callers were rank beginners. To them my relatively long experience made me an "expert." They expected to hear from me a recipe for success. A few years earlier I might have been able to recite it for them with confidence, but by now I knew how complex the equation for success in winemaking really is. Sure, I could tell them what to do about mildew and how to get the fermentation finished and where to find supplies and what varieties of grapes would probably grow well in their region and even give them some help in designing their winery. What kept me awake more often than not, after they had hung up, were the questions they *hadn't* asked, and the question in my own mind: "Should I have volunteered the answers to them anyway?"

There is a certain note one can hear between the lines in another's conversation which conveys deep sincerity, and when I heard this note coupled with beginner's questions about winemaking I could imagine myself in the other person's position and I would wonder whether I had an obligation to say that for him—not for everybody, but for him, or her—winemaking could be dangerously addictive and many many things besides those inquired about should be considered before going any further. "Can you afford it?" Roland had asked me, and I had to admit that I had wished often that I had *really* understood the importance of that question in my beginning days. The really important subjects for discussion, I felt, were impossible to broach: "Can your marriage take the strain?" for example, is one I would have asked if I dared. "Have you drunk enough good wine to know what you're doing?" was another. How impertinent that would have sounded to most of my callers!

The question of which grape varieties to plant was one that was asked regularly, and usually with great urgency because of the controversy between the pure-vinifera believers and the hybrid enthusiasts. I never learned to answer it simply. I can unequivocally say that I have no personal preferences between the two categories: hybrid and vinifera. I have tasted more wines I prefer that were made from vinifera. I believe this to be true because there are more fine winemakers in the world who have only vinifera to work with. In eastern American regions, where both categories are equally available, I have found the average quality of wines made from each to be equal. Almost without exception I have found that my qualitative preferences are more dependent upon the ability of the winemaker than the characteristics of the grape.

Keep in mind that there is a greater fund of knowledge and experience available to users of the older (vinifera) grape varieties than for the hybrids. It therefore calls for less talent and dedication to make an acceptable wine from them. If good-quality vinifera grapes are available to a reasonably good winemaker it will be simpler for him to make a wine from them that will have the flavor and characteristics associated with known good wines. If he comes even close to imitating those known wines, he will be praised by those whose estimation of quality depends upon established parameters.

I confess that I get greater pleasure and satisfaction from wines that are excellent and unique, representing the initiative, judgment, and personal goal of the producer, than I do from those that merely remind me of other wines.

To my callers I must have frequently sounded indecisive. So much depended upon very personal characteristics of the questioner, which I couldn't possibly know, but I often wished that I dared to risk sounding "preachy" and paraphrase an impromptu lecture given to me once by an old Burgundian. The objective of his impassioned discourse was to express disdain for the impudence of young winemakers, especially Californians who, just out of school with their degree in Oenology, were challenging the great wines of Burgundy in blind tastings. "So they can grow a pinot noir."

He shrugged, indignant. "Un noble cépage can no more insure the production of a fine wine than a fine piano can
guarantee fine music! Even with the highest-trained winemaker, with all the technology of the modern world at his
fingertips, one cannot automatically expect great wine.
Écoutez-moi, imagine that we are in a concert hall. Paderewski approaches a magnificent grand piano twelve feet long,
sweeps aside the tails of his coat, sits down, and lifts his
hands to strike a chord. Are we guaranteed a fine musical
experience? Pas, absolument. Une troisième chose, ingrédient essentiel se manque . . . the music itself. Without great
music the splendid piano, the talented maestro are merely
tools. It is only by the addition of a great purpose that these
tools can produce something truly fine.

"Similarly a splendid grape and a well-trained and
equipped winemaker are dependent on a third ingredient to
make a great wine. There must be a great . . . goal. The
winemaker must have an objective in his mind—even in the
taste buds of his mouth—as he considers the materials
which the vine has given him. Malheureusement, the means
for achieving this goal cannot be written down like the notes
of music. It must exist as an idea, and that idea, mon vieux,
can only be formed by the experience of drinking good wine.
Lots of it. Years of it . . . What good is a fine grape to a
winemaker who has only experienced soda pop?"

Even though this tirade was inspired perhaps by a certain amount of professional jealousy, there was a message in
it of importance. The momentum of small-winery growth
east of California has never abated but the chaotic search for
professional guidance fortunately sparked a response from
various other sources than us relatively few pioneer farm
winemakers alone. The New York State Agricultural Experiment Station at Geneva was by this time able to offer periodic seminars in the fundamentals of winemaking to supplement an already well-developed literature on grape growing.
The neighboring state of Pennsylvania had in fact anticipated New York in permitting the licensing of limited-

production wineries and had organized an excellent annual grape and wine conference, which provided basic training for hundreds of beginning winemakers.

The American Wine Society had, for years, been contributing significantly to a fundamental understanding of winemaking and continued to do so with periodic seminars also. All of these seminars or conferences served more than the need for basic training. As the numbers of participants in the fledgling industry grew they also provided a place for the winemakers of all levels to meet and exchange ideas, to taste each other's wines and by doing so to shape their own goals more sensibly. This goal-shaping function was an extremely important one. Less than a dozen of the hundreds of new winemakers had anything faintly resembling professional experience. Only a few more had a wine-drinking experience extending over more than three or four years. This lack of taste experience unfortunately included most of the technological experts at the conference. The number of us who had a background of as much as fifteen or twenty years during which the regular consumption of a wide selection of truly good European wines had had a chance to shape our judgment of wine, and thus our winemaking goals, was limited to a handful.

Looking back and considering the generally amateur level of experience, I believe the level of wine quality at the early conferences was remarkably high. There were, to be sure, some disappointing ones. This shouldn't have been a surprise, but it was. Somehow I think that those of us who had so ardently backed the farm-winery legislation had made ourselves believe that since it was the big eastern wineries that had ruined the region's winemaking reputation with their sweet grapy confections, the small producers, able to put their hearts into their winemaking ahead of their pocketbooks, would just naturally do everything right. We learned that small was not automatically beautiful.

Nevertheless, the spirit of intense interest which pervaded at the time seemed to make these conferences extremely effective learning experiences. The second year the wines as a whole were vastly improved. By the third, wine- makers who had previously been doctors, farmers, business executives, or students were making technically excellent wines. I'm deliberately hedging a bit by saying "technically" excellent. I mean by that term that their fermentations were well managed, the wines were clean-tasting, not oxidized, limpid. Those things about wine which could be learned from books had in most cases been well learned. In an aston- ishingly short time the infant industry was ready to go to market with something close to five million gallons of American wine far better than had ever before been made east of California. But now its problem had shifted from how to make wine to how to sell it.

During this period a fourth conference had been orga- nized, this time as a proprietorial operation created by a young man named William Moffett. Bill first turned his efforts toward the publication of a magazine for wine pro- ducers to serve the needs of what he knew would be a vital new industry. As an extension of this project he organized an educational seminar similar to those already functioning and added various marketing-oriented features, which were well timed to address the needs of the new industry. He charged a fee for his seminar, placed it in a large well- equipped hotel, attracted first-rate lecturers from the aca- demic field as well as from the growing industry itself. He offered a wine competition and invited well-qualified wine writers to judge it, with the clear hopes that the judges themselves would become a part of a promotional effort to gain the new eastern wineries a better recognition among consumers. He also persuaded manufacturers of equipment for grape growing and winemaking to exhibit their wares. All aspects of Bill's projects were well timed to succeed and, although I'm sure there were some difficult financing prob- lems, both his magazine, *The Eastern Grape Grower*, and his seminar survived them to provide a major organizational force for the benefit of the industry.

chapter X

The Bottom Line

The marketing problems facing the new eastern winemakers were horrendous. As a rule they had no money for advertising. Many had spent their life savings and gone deeply into debt to build their wineries. Few knew much about marketing anyway. Most of their marketing efforts had evolved to one degree or another into making their wineries a kind of entertainment attraction; they sold their wines on premises to tourists attracted by the age-old allure of seeing wine made and the prospect of a free drink. Some wineries became so involved in their entertainment activities that their winemaking became secondary. Bill Moffett envisioned a widespread promotional campaign of national scope to create a general background of consumer recognition and interest in eastern wines, with which wineries, no matter what the scope of their individual or local promotional efforts, could identify themselves.

With some exceptions most of the small eastern wineries recognized that their major marketing hurdle was this matter of identification. In a way it was more a matter of dis-identification. It was essential that they separate, in the consumer's mind, their new table-wine productions from the old style of wines, those sweet grapy confections of the big, established eastern wineries.

Bill hoped to finance his promotion through a wide association of small wineries with generally similar marketing objectives and similar styles of wines. They would pay for the promotion collectively through an assessment based on the volume of their production and wine sales. Unfortunately the total volume of the young industry was still so small that no reasonable per-gallon assessment could produce enough money to fund a promotion of sufficient impact to justify its cost. Bill and his business partner in the publishing business, an attractive, energetic young woman, Hope Merletti, displayed enormous initiative and imagination in their efforts to get their plan underway. In doing so they gained the widespread admiration of the small wineries —and even the somewhat wary respect of the big established wineries. Encouraged by this, Bill and Hope began to postulate the idea of a cooperative promotional effort, jointly funded by the little wineries and the big ones.

However, the purists among the small producers (which included Benmarl) felt extremely uncomfortable with the thought of forming a marketing association with the very producers whose products we were so eager to disassociate from our own. We needn't have been uneasy. The big wineries upon whom the major portion of the funding would have fallen were quite definitely opposed to increasing their already overwhelming competition from California and Europe by supporting the growth of this new disorganized, rambunctious group of would-be competitors.

Their reluctance was understandable. The so-called

"wine press," which had either ignored or criticized their wines had apparently been captivated by these new impecunious idealists. It seemed that you could hardly open a newspaper or magazine at that time which didn't have an article praising Benmarl, Dr. Frank, or Bully Hill and by implication, or directly, disparaging the big wineries. Articles about Bully Hill must have been the worst to endure. Its owner, Walter Taylor, had actually been one of their top executives, indeed the heir apparent of the mighty Taylor Wine Company. He had left the company, according to report, because of a difference of opinion regarding their winemaking practices, then had repurchased his grandfather's original grape farm, known as Bully Hill, and built himself a new winery. Any news story about Walter was as colorful as he is himself. Given the forum of a news story or a feature article he lit into the company his family had founded with the vigorous invective that only a family vendetta could inspire. His criticisms of the Taylor Wine Company spilled over onto all the rest of the old establishment wineries.

I agreed and sympathized with Walter. The difficulties of trying to establish a winery and to encourage an industry devoted to making wines of high quality in eastern America were multiplied a thousandfold by the burden of the region's past reputation. The frustrations of trying to overcome it kept my adrenaline level almost as high as his. Even though my own efforts to advance the interests of eastern winemaking were successful and rewarding, my role could never be that of the fiery, sword-wielding warrior that Walter was, and I frankly envied him.

Bill Moffett was an idealist, too. I knew that from our long friendship. When he started his magazine I half expected, and hoped, that he like Walter would use his polished, articulate talent to boldly attack the wineries and the practices that had brought eastern wine to its present low status. Perhaps he would have done so if he had continued to publish his magazine alone, but *The Eastern Grape Grower,* as a co-production, took a more pragmatic and conservative posture. I excused them. They had a living to make, I rationalized, and therefore had to seek a way to serve the interests of *all* the elements of the eastern wine industry. This explained, I thought, their interest in trying to form a marketing coalition between two factions I considered to be inevitably locked in combat until one was destroyed.

Bill and Hope's sweet reasonableness plagued me. I wanted to fight! The rascals who had defeated my first efforts toward farm wineries twenty years earlier were still the enemies of progress. And yet, doggone it all, I had to admit that a unified wine industry could achieve so many things a fractionated one could not. I was not able to see any way it could find a common marketing goal, but there were certainly many legal restrictions and other restraints impinging unfairly on all winemakers, which could more effectively be addressed by a large unified organization.

This conflict between the urge to join Walter or to opt for cooperation and join Bill kept me awake at night. I had already planned a course for Benmarl of actively criticizing the old New York wine establishment, which I knew could lead to open confrontation with it. I had convinced myself that I had a moral obligation to do everything I could to expose it as aesthetically barren, financially greedy, and unfairly exploitative of the state's grape farmers, whose crops —which they had an obligation and sometimes contractual agreements to buy—were rotting on the vine while they bought California wines, blended them with theirs, and sold them as New York wines. Now I had serious doubts that attacking the big wineries would serve the cause of small wine producers.

The conflict was to become a crisis of conscience before I resolved it. For many months I had been trying to persuade the producers of public television's *MacNeil-Lehrer Report,* an in-depth news program, to devote a show to the subject of America's growing interest in wine and to let me take part to emphasize the importance that the new farm wineries would have in this development. More recently I had suggested that the plight of New York's grape farmers vis-à-vis the big wineries deserved a debate on their show. This had sparked some interest, but instead I was invited to take part in a program devoted to a general discussion of wine topics, such as how to read and understand the information on wine labels, and so on.

Disappointed, I nevertheless accepted the invitation. It would be easy to make light conversation of such trivia. But what a waste of time when such issues as I had proposed could and should be aired! In the back of my mind, as I flew down to the Washington studio for the broadcast, the thought formed that during the course of the program the opportunity would arise for me at least to mention my controversial issues—perhaps even throw down the gauntlet of challenge. On a nationally televised show it might draw enough response to arouse public indignation and win sympathy for the David and Goliath struggle of small eastern wineries against the oppressive giants of their industry.

But what if I succeeded in making a national issue of the controversy, embarrassing the established wineries? They would still not be likely to change their practices. They were not, after all, doing anything illegal. The simple fact that they were not making as good wines as I thought they could make was a business decision totally their own. The fact that they were not honoring their responsibilities to support their regional grape growers was a matter for the grape growers to deal with, and was likewise none of my business. Benmarl was not affected directly by any of these matters. Even its market was well insulated from the spillover of New York's low-quality image. Our clients were almost entirely private subscribers, sophisticated and aware that our wines were not typical of New York.

The only excuse I had for inserting myself into this issue was a certain sense of responsibility for the welfare of small winemakers because I had encouraged and sponsored the farm-winery concept. I had already learned that not all of them were great winemakers simply by reason of being small. Perhaps some of them might even want to make their wines by the methods I was about to disparage. The truth was that I was thinking like, and about to act like, a busybody do-gooder. I would probably accomplish nothing except to widen the gap between the factions of industry that Bill and Hope were trying to narrow.

By air time I was so hopelessly ensnared on the horns of my self-created dilemma that I sat dumbly through the broadcast, unable to contribute more than a few optimistic words about the great future for wine in America. I'm certain that my performance was a disappointment to the show's producer. It was a disappointment to me too because I learned that when push came to shove I wasn't really the gladiator type. I would have to leave that kind of work to others. Shortly afterward I threw my support, for whatever it was worth, to Bill's efforts. He was able with the help of Peter Karp, then Widmer's Wine Cellars' board chairman, to put together a strong coalition of wineries of all sizes and winemaking persuasions, called AAV, the Association of American Vintners. I was asked to serve on its board of directors.

AAV, however, was not organized as a marketing instrument as Bill had originally envisioned it, for the same reasons that were mentioned earlier: the small wineries had to spend all their money on local promotion and the big wineries saw no reason to fund the development of competition.

The need of the small wineries for general marketing assistance, however, was just as acute as ever. Perhaps more so. As their numbers grew their newsworthiness diminished. It was becoming harder and harder to get the wonderful free publicity afforded earlier by the media. Everyone had already done a wine story. What else was new? An idea came from an unexpected source.

Bill McDevitt represented the interests of New York's Metropolitan Package Store Association as their executive director, an activity that included the close observation of political events that might affect these merchants. This made it necessary for him to spend a lot of time in Albany. Ever since I had gotten involved in the farm-winery legislation I seemed to find myself there quite frequently too.

Since small wineries now outnumbered the big ones, we had a kind of political status and our attitudes toward legislative issues, etc., was a matter of some curiosity.

For example, McDevitt, in the interests of the wine merchants, wished to discourage a proposed modification of New York statutes which would permit wines to be sold in New York grocery stores. New York had, in fact, been rather tardy in permitting this type of wine sale. California and most other states had long since done so. At first glance it would seem that, since we were the second-largest wine-producing state in the union, the establishment wineries would have long since removed this apparent barrier to increased sales. Some said that the reason they had not was that a determined and powerful lobby of retail wine merchants had sufficient clout to prevent it. There was also a point of view which held that the New York wineries were willing to preserve the status quo because opening up this vast new market outlet would expose them to vastly increased competition from California and other out-of-state producers. The question of where farm wineries, whose political constituency was spread through the state, would come down on this matter, obviously concerned McDevitt.

For once I found myself embarrassingly on the same side of a controversy as the New York establishment. It seemed to me that the massive increase in wine outlets that would result from permitting sales in grocery stores would simply swamp the small wineries with competition they couldn't stand up to. They were not yet producing sufficient volume to supply such a mass market. Their cost structure at this point in their development prevented them from being competitive in price. Even if they somehow got space on a supermarket shelf they had no advertising budget.

Their brands would not have a chance of public recognition in the vast jungle of the food market. My feelings about this matter were shared by my fellow producers in the Hudson River region and the same point of view seemed to represent a consensus among the upstate wineries as well.

McDevitt had an idea for raising advertising money which he thought the retail merchants would support in exchange for support of their position opposing wine in grocery stores—"an excise tax of a fraction of a penny on every bottle of wine sold in the State of New York. It wouldn't hurt anybody and could produce something like $400,000 a year." Properly used by a state agency, such a fund could provide an advertising backup for *all* New York wines, which could help the merchants to get a disillusioned public to try them again.

As the concept took shape various factions in the industry became uneasy about who would administer the spending of the money. Were the farm wineries going to take this bonanza and use it to build a halo around themselves at the expense of the establishment? Where would the grape growers, who had not become farm wineries, fit in? They still had to sell all the grapes they could to the big wineries. What kind of advertising would be created? Who would decide? Should the package stores have a say in it? What about allocating part of the money toward research at the Agricultural Experiment Station? Finally, a proposal that a committee composed of all these factions should advise the state's governor who would administer the fund won general approval. All factions retired to select their committee representatives.

The New York wine industry met in Binghamton and nominated a steering committee of four people chosen to represent the interests of the various-sized wineries: Ernest Herzog, whose Royal Wine Company produced about a million-and-a-half gallons; Ted Cribari of the Barry Wine Company, something over 200,000 gallons; Bert Silk, vice president of the Canandaigua Wine Company, whose pro-

duction of 12 million gallons made it the second biggest in
New York. The question of who would represent the small
wineries hung suspensefully over the meeting. Walter Taylor of Bully Hill was the most likely candidate, but word had
been circulated that if he were elected all the big wineries
would walk out in protest. Walter understood the importance of his position. Joseph Swarthout, president of the
Taylor Wine Company, Walter's arch enemy, stood up. "I
would like to nominate Mark Miller as the fourth committee
member." He sat down.

Walter stood up. "I second the nomination."

Silk laid down the committee's ground rules from the
first meeting. If the wineries in his production class were to
permit themselves to participate in this scheme, it must be
understood that this committee would agree, first, to com-
pose a plan for a realistically represented association of New
York wine producers. "Realistic" meant that the organization would be composed of regional directors elected periodically by their regional peers; each would have the same
voting power, but the four largest producers in the state
would have, in addition, four appointed directors not subject to election. This organization, insisted Silk, would elect
representatives to the governor's committee. It was a tough,
"play it this way or the game is off" proposal. But it was fair,
and I had to face it, it was the only game in town. Without
the big wineries participating, the prospects of creating the
fund were hopeless.

Our committee of four met many times before the
mechanism of this plan could be perfected and accepted by
our own regional constituents. No one was overjoyed. Although the four of us who had worked our way through the
details of the plan had come to trust and like each other, our
constituencies feared they would be led to an agreement
which might be a dangerous compromise. To the big producers $400,000 would obviously mean very little for their
overall advertising strategies. It was hardly worth their time
to join. To the farm wineries, the sum, although large com-

pared to their combined advertising expenditures, was still pitifully inadequate to mount a major campaign. Worse still, and this troubled me a great deal, by joining our former enemies we were tacitly agreeing to stop criticizing them— perhaps our most effective means of attracting attention from the media. Our David-against-Goliath posture would have to be abandoned.

In spite of the reservations of all parties, however, the plan was accepted, regional directors were chosen, and their first meeting was convened in Albany. Our steering committee reported its assignment completed and the elected directors were seated. Officers were elected. President Bert Silk announced the first order of business to be the acceptance of the excise-tax promotional fund and asked for a motion to that effect. The motion was made and seconded.

Although unanimous agreement was assumed, a roll-call vote seemed appropriate on this symbolic matter. The organization existed only because of it. It was apparent that a considerable sense of pride of accomplishment was felt by each director as he said a quiet yes, or nodded smiling. At no time in the past had the New York wine industry ever been so unified. The regionally-elected directors all voted. It was the turn of the top-volume producers, who had permanent seats on the committee. For Canandaigua, Bert Silk nodded "aye." It was Taylor's turn. I turned toward their representative, a tall, mild-mannered, extremely likable young man, who had only recently come into the Taylor Wine Company, when it was purchased by Coca-Cola. He puffed on his pipe only for an instant before speaking, but it was enough to break the smooth cadence of assenting votes. "No," he said quietly.

Silence fell over the room. All eyes turned questioningly to him. His shoulders shrugged almost imperceptibly as he looked levelly back at our surprised faces. "No."

It took a few moments for anyone to speak or perhaps it only seemed that way to me. Finally conversation resumed. "Why?" He didn't say very much. He was simply representing his company's position. A cold, helpless anger crept slowly over me. Taylor! My old nemesis. Fair or not, this company was, to me, the dinosaur of the wine industry, stepping heavily, implacably, ruthlessly on every effort to bring eastern winemaking out of the ice age.

Like a plague, I fumed, returning every so often to impede whatever advances had been made since its last assault. At the thought of the word "plague" my memory jumped back to an evening shortly after we had bought Benmarl. Dene and I were invited to dine at a friend's home in Hartsdale with Margaret Mead, the world-renowned anthropologist. Inconveniently I had to deliver an illustration that afternoon before the dinner. I hurriedly finished it and rushed it into New York with just enough time to dash home to dress for dinner. Unfortunately, the art director wasn't entirely pleased and insisted on some minor changes. As the picture had to go directly to the engraver's there was nothing to be done except to correct the painting then and there.

I telephoned Dene to go ahead without me since we were to provide the wine for the evening, and to explain to our hosts that I would try to be only a few minutes late. By the time I actually arrived, the moments had become nearly an hour. My hostess's delicately timed dinner had been hopelessly disarranged, but in spite of Dene's urging to begin dining without me she graciously insisted on waiting. I think she really wanted to use me as a sort of anthropological phenomenon for the famous Dr. Mead to comment on: "Exhibit A, homo suburbiae," example of how the soft, well-ordered life of suburban culture with all its creature comforts still could not prevent certain odd apostates from deserting for unknown, certainly less comfortable adventures, like farming.

By the time I arrived my tardiness and my idiosyncrasies had become the focus of the conversation. Embarrassed, I apologized profusely to my hosts and to Dr. Mead, blurting out an excuse to the effect that such work deadlines and the pressure of a career that kept one lurching from crisis to crisis in the urban rat race were the very things that had made me buy a farm and commence a return to the peaceful rural life of my childhood. The other guests smiled sympathetically but Dr. Mead looked at me gravely and said, "And what will you do if a plague of locusts comes along, Mr. Miller?" The question was assumed by the group to be rhetorical and so I joined the laughter instead of attempting to answer.

Of course the "plague of locusts" had come along— many times, in many forms: bird damage; the defeat of my first farm-winery campaign by Taylor; VDI; once an actual plague of locustlike insects that preferred to eat tree leaves but, since they weren't available, found grape leaves equally tasty. Each time we had either met and driven off the "plague" or hunkered in and waited till it passed. This latest manifestation would also yield eventually as the others had done.

During the following weeks, I did what I could to combat the Taylor Wine Company's opposition and so did many others, but the legislation which would have created the promotional fund for New York wines was quietly defeated. There was one small consolation. There was now a real New York wine industry organization where before there had been only an unrelated collection of New York wineries. The New York State Wine Producer's Association now existed. The industry had a voice. It would just have to wait a while longer to find something it could say.

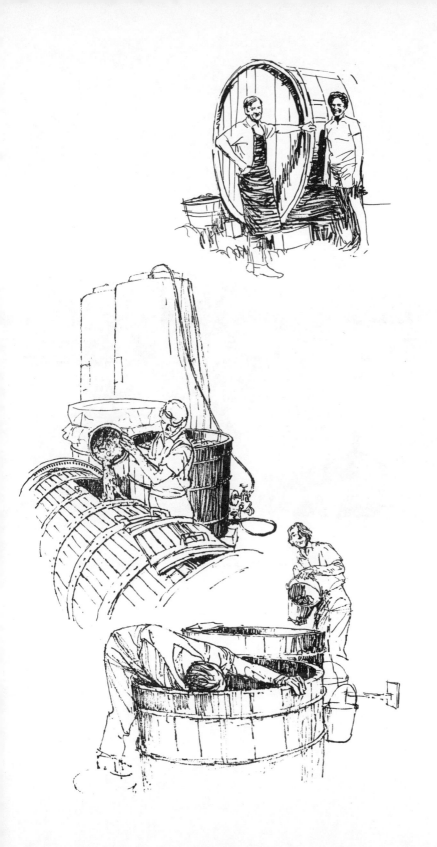

Epilogue

This book is not going to come to an end with the story completed and Benmarl sitting on her hill, the crown jewel of a totally replanted Hudson River wine region, its family of dedicated *vignerons* clustered at the feet of a silver-haired *patron,* recounting their struggles from the day when there were only High Tor and Benmarl in New York, pressing out the first trickle of a river of wine acclaimed as the peer of the realm.

It is, instead, going to have to end rather arbitrarily almost in mid-paragraph. The intensity of our nation's interest in wine is accelerating so rapidly there is just not enough time to write any more right now. Oh, Benmarl sits smiling on her hill, her vineyards are green, her cellars are full of good wine—26,000 gallons were made last year, in fact—but the *patron* is too busy planting new vineyards and seeking ways to make more wine because of the explosion of interest in it in our nation.

Wine has become very important to many Americans. We are becoming a country of mealtime wine consumers much more rapidly than even my optimism had envisioned, doing it, in characteristically American fashion, in great gulps instead of sips. Moreover, we are drinking increasing amounts of wine grown in our own native soils as well as (and frequently in preference to) wines originating in famous old-world regions. This acceptance of our own wines has come about during the years encompassed by the story I have told you up to here.

Of course dozens of such stories as ours could have been told of this period and hopefully they will be told. This accomplishment has only been made possible by the dedication and determination of people who have demonstrated that fine winemaking, both as an art and as a business, is well within the capabilities of our nation's climates, soils, and talents. Hundreds more adventures are in process now and perhaps will also eventually become part of the legend of the difficulties and rewards experienced in eventually making America "wine country."

As I write it is Labor Day. This week we will begin picking the vintage of '82. I awoke this morning before five, put on my robe, tiptoed out of the bedroom, hoping not to wake Dene, and started walking across the courtyard to my studio, determined to finish this book so as to put my mind completely to the harvest. A high wall of bright-hued plastic grape-picking trays were stacked neatly near the processing area of the winery, waiting for harvesting to begin. A tray had fallen into the roadway and I went over to pick it up. Not nearly so picturesque, I thought, as the old-fashioned wooden bushel baskets we used in the early days. "Sentimentalist!" I chided myself. "They're far easier to clean. Anyway, in a few years' time there will be machine harvesters capable of handling even steep terrains like Benmarl, and all picking baskets will be out of date.

The sugar content of our grapes is rising very nearly one degree per day, and by Thursday, or perhaps sooner if the weather continues hot and dry, we will begin picking the Seyval grapes for white wine. Our picking crews, composed of volunteer Société members and local professionals, will cut the ripe grapes from the vines and leave filled baskets of them under the vine trellises to be consolidated into bins and carted to the winery. I turned to walk past the processing area. Here they will be weighed, destemmed, and crushed, the juice pumped immediately up through a large hose to the gleaming yellow horizontal press. Lab tests will confirm the

field tests of the sugar level of the grape juice, which will already be flowing freely into the 8-inch deep tray beneath the press.

When it is full the press will be closed and its two electrically driven end plates will gently squeeze out something between 160 and 175 gallons per ton of grapes. With the equipment we now have, more could be obtained by further pressing, but the quality of the additional juice

would be less fine. The juice will be inoculated with a selected strain of yeast to convert the grape sugars into alcohol
with more assurance than the wild yeasts which are naturally present on the grape's skin.

A few days later the estate's early-ripening red wine
grapes will be given much the same treatment, except that
after destemming they will be pumped into stainless-steel
tanks and fermented there in contact with their dark skins
until sufficient color, tannin, and various other qualities
have been extracted by maceration in the increasingly alcoholic must. At least twice daily a cap of grape skins, carried
to the top of the violently fermenting juice by bubbles of

escaping carbon dioxide, a by-product of fermentation, will
be submerged by pumping over it wine drawn from the
bottom of the tank. Depending upon the intensity of extrac-
tion desired, the reds will be pressed after four to twelve
days, and their fragrant purple juice will flow into tall stainless tanks—as had the whites—in what we call the fermenting room, adjoining the processing pit.

I peered into one of the line of gleaming tanks. Here all

the wines would finish their alcoholic fermentation and over a period of a few weeks the roiling, seething liquid would become tranquil and the tiny floating particles of skins, seeds, and yeast cells would gradually succumb to the pull of gravity and sink, forming a thick sediment on the bottom of the tank. The clearing wine would then be racked into a fresh container, leaving the deposited sediment behind. This process would be repeated numerous times over the next few months, until the wine was limpid, or if there was reason for more rapid clearing the solid matter could be removed by filtration. Although this quite simple series of events would only take two and a half to three months, many critical management decisions would have been made during the period which would have unalterably determined the basic character of the wine. Probably no two winemakers would have achieved exactly the same results.

I stepped into the main barrel-storage area. Double-tiered rows of small, fifty- to sixty-five-gallon wooden casks lined the walls, with another row running through the center of the room. Only about half the wines in the tank room would be brought in here for a five- to ten-month storage in these expensive white-oak barrels. Those which were would be changed significantly during their stay by absorption of tannins and woody flavors from the barrels and also by the slow absorption of oxygen through the pores of the wood. The young fragrant wines that entered the barrels would become less fruity in aroma, more austere and complex in flavor. They would not necessarily be better for this change, but youthful charm would have been exchanged for more mature grace. Both characteristics have their special value and each has a special use with different foods. I have a personal bias favoring the nutty and vanilla-like character of oak-stored wines, both red and white, for accompaniment of most food, but I favor the simpler, more vivacious qualities of non-oaked wines for apéritif use or for picnics and sandwich luncheons.

I was rather proud of this room and what it has represented in our search for more interesting wines. Six different

forests were represented in our collection of oaks. The use
of small new oak cooperage as the Europeans use it had
almost disappeared in the "high-tech" period of American
winemaking during which we had returned to America in
1967. So had the use of malo-lactic-acid conversion. Our
winemaking methods, including these, had been shared by
a very small phalanx of foresighted winemakers, who had
the humility to use hindsight in searching for better ways to
make wine.

A dim glow of light ahead led me into the adjoining
room. Someone had forgotten to turn off a light in the winery "museum." The museum occupies a corner of the room,
enclosed by iron bars guarding our collection of wines dat-
ing back to the first year of our licensed operation in 1971.
Since all wines in it are "out-of-bond," or tax paid, we also
keep there our collection of other winemakers' wines—a
bottle or so of Monsieur Noblé's La Romanée, Henri Latour's excellent Auxey-Duresses 1961—a few sentimental
treasures such as a gallon jar of wild cherry wine, 1958, and
more important Benmarl's red blend of Baco Noir and Maréchal Foch, both French-American hybrids of 1971, which,

poured unidentified for connoisseurs, had repeatedly been presumed to be a fine old Burgundian wine.

My little detour had drawn me through the winery in reverse order of the construction of its numerous additions. Starting with the new hydraulic grape reception station, moving through the tank and barrel rooms, where we expected to make something like 26,000 gallons of wine of this 1982 harvest and begin its processing alongside approximately the same amount of wine just now beginning to be consumed as the last of the '80s disappeared, I had made my way to the case storage room. There is always a pang of . . . well, perhaps jealousy is the word, when the last of any vintage is sold—all winemakers seem to feel it. "C'est préférable à donner mon sang à moi (my own blood) than to part with the last bottle of a favorite vintage," I had heard many say.

Usually a portion of a successful bottling gets squirreled away in the winery museum, but sometimes there is a frustrating slip-up. For example, a few weeks ago Arlen Lessin, a Société member of many years' standing, had called to say that he wished to make a business courtesy gift to Baron Guy de Rothschild, proprietor of the renowned Château Lafite. "Would you mind," he asked, "if I gave him a bottle of my Benmarl wine?" I gulped, a little taken aback by his bold suggestion. We conversationally rifled his cellar and discovered he had some Cuvée 9A of 1979, and he decided to send it. When Monsieur Rothschild responded to Arlen with a charming handwritten note praising the wine—"No California wine can compete with it"—I scurried around the winery, searching for more to store away in the museum. With such a brilliant recognition in its youth surely this wine must be destined for a fabulous old age. But no more could be found.

I walked through the tasting room. This had originally been the receiving station, the press room, the fermentation room, the barrel room, the bottle-storage area—the lot. All two hundred gallons of it. We were certainly not a big winery even now by comparison with the giants of California, but we had come a long way, and Baron Rothschild's note supported my boast that we and other eastern wineries were tweaking the giants' noses and might yet fulfill the prediction in *Time* magazine of "Shaking California's Throne." It would take a few investment dollars to do it but we would find them. There must be some others out there with both courage and the means to join us in putting Benmarl into its next expansion phase. I smiled, recalling a wine writer's wry comment in a recent magazine article, "Want to make a small fortune in the wine business?" he asked. "Start with a large fortune and build a winery." It was Roland's "genteelman's game" restated in Americanese. But what a great adventure it has been! What is worth doing that has no risk?

It was beginning to be light outside as I closed the winery door behind me and directed my steps again to the studio. I looked toward the eastern sky, rosy pink just before sunrise. The "dragon" was on the river. "A good sign," I said to myself. The "dragon" appears at times of seasonal weather change. It is caused by a layer of fog that forms on the cool surface of the deep Hudson River toward dawn; when the sun rises over the foothills of the Berkshires its heat lifts the fog off the water's surface, forming a long undulating coil, which slowly moves in the direction of the receding tide toward the south. Centipede-like legs of fog steadily dropped and lifted as if it were stalking a prey. The round red ball of the sun became a fierce eye as it rose through the dragon's yawing head and a white tongue flicked toward an early-moving tugboat, which hooted back defiantly. "A good sign." Cool nights, hot sunny days hasten the sugar development in the grapes and deepen their color. I sharpened my pencil and went to work.

It has been lovely weather. Cloudless. A bright September sun bathing the green vines. There has hardly been a sound except for an occasional bang of the bird cannons. I haven't seen a bird. The cicadas haven't yet begun their summer-ending drone. Some friends who have been Société members for eight years dropped by about noon to pick up some wine and showed us their new Volvo, which George has just bought to celebrate his retirement. We loaded ten cases of wine into his trunk, enough to hold them until they can return later this fall. The Société now has more than a thousand members, who sponsor more than fifteen hundred vinerights—a magnificently thirsty lot, their numbers still growing! Each member *"Vigneron"* is as proud as I am of the work we have done together. Prouder sometimes, I think, because they consider only the things we have accomplished and are not concerned so much as I am by the work there is still to do.

They have watched the beginning of a profound cultural change in America and helped Benmarl evolve in that milieu from a quirky hobby to a position of pride and responsible leadership in a new industry which it played a part in creating. For me, the thousands of acres of this magnificent Hudson Valley waiting to be replanted with wine grapes dominates my thoughts, and the hundreds of thousands of bottles of Hudson region wine which are yet to be made. I took a bottle of our wine to France with me last month. At Benmarl we call it a "sparkling" or *crémant* wine but it is made sparkling just as fine champagne is made by a second fermentation in the bottle. I opened it to the delighted surprise of a friend in Reims whom I would like to help finance a venture to expand Benmarl's production of all its wines, which will include sparkling wines like this grown in the Hudson region. He knows that France cannot hope to supply the enormous demand the world is already making for fine champagne-quality wines. He also knows that California's bland climate produces grapes generally lacking the acidity balance which is essential for the best wines of this type.

"Cet étonnant ce vin!" he said as I poured a second glass.

"Join me," I invited. "Eastern America, the Hudson

Valley, will be the site of the next great spurt of growth in the world's wine industry."

The sun is just sinking behind the trees on the west side of Benmarl's courtyard. The shadow of our "château," designed by Dene, falls across the vineyard terraces. The valley looks, in the evening light, very much as I saw it for the first time twenty-six years ago. I wonder what Andrew Caywood would think of our efforts during those years. Another season is nearly over, but in a few days Benmarl's cellars will be buzzing with the fermentation of new wine, the very essence of this year, a wine in the making that will reflect in its character every drop of refreshing rain, every bright warm day of its season of conception. Whether it is destined to be great or insignificant it will always preserve a little of its store of sunshine for some of our future days.

The future unwinding of that destiny will provide an interesting continuation of this story, whoever takes up a pencil to write it. I hope it is I who will do it, and that before its little drama is fully played and its final curtain drawn, you will be among the cast of players yourself.

To those of you fellow *vignerons* in our little Société des Vignerons, which has made this adventure possible, a most cordial "thank you" for the pleasure of your company so far. In the words of François Rabelais, a toast to all of us winemakers: "Quand nos verres serront plein les viderons, et quand ils serront vide les pleindrons encore!"*

---

*When our glasses are full let us empty them . . . and when they are empty let us fill them again.